26 DREAMS

26 DREAMS

Emmanuel "Gift" Clack

DEDICATION

I dedicate this book to Lois Marie Clack. The single most important person in my life. You were the first person to love me, the first person to encourage me. The first person to tell me I could do anything in life. The first person to tell me I had a Gift. You told me to be fearless, go after the things I want and to walk with God. I listened to you moma. I hear your voice guiding me every step of the way. My life goal is to continue to hear you say "I'm proud of you my son."

ACKNOWLEDGEMENTS

This is for Louisville, KY.

CONTENTS

PROLOGUE

When's the last time you thought about dying?

Like really thought about it, like down to the minute-by-minute details.

Who would be there?

Where it would be?

How you'd want it to go?

Have you ever thought that in depth about it?

I'm cautious to not categorize it as an obsession, but I eagerly anticipate dying. Wait. Let me forewarn you. This isn't a cry for help. I'm not going to detail my disdain for life and speak of its ills and how I wish to escape it. No. This is about how I realized that life isn't important. Death is. Death is for certain. At this point, it's just a formality. Nobody will remember your life if you die for nothing. That being said, it's become my life goal to not die in vain.

Don't let me.

How you live will not extend past your death if you never broker your death. How do you broker your death? Easy. By leaving a legacy. Those remembered, in time, are those who excelled, reached their dreams, and those whose death left a profound effect; albeit from failures or success. I'm brokering my death to that of success. Everyday I've fighting for my dreams. Everyday I'm fighting towards my goal. Everyday I'm walking in my purpose. Everyday I'm defining my destiny to ensure that when

I die, my death is used to exemplify a success story. I don't want to be forgotten.

I want to die and live forever.

Have you ever died before? I have.

I've killed myself on multiple occasions.

How close have you been to taking your own life?

Have you ever attempted to end your life?
Think aloud to yourself.

What were those experiences like?

How did it change you?

How did it affect you?

In my opinion, if you've never tried to kill yourself or lost your will or desire to live, then you've never lived. Extreme? Maybe. But to me, it's practical. Imagine going through school never having to take a test.

How would you pass?

Tests are necessary, primarily so that you can know the progress you've made to that point. We're all familiar with the cliché: "Life is a test."

How do we grade that test?

What scale are the results to be measured with?

Who the heck knows? I'm not a fan of standards and prototypical avenues in which life should go or pan out. In my life, (and I'm sure in yours) I've been tested numerous times and only in hindsight am I able to grade myself. If you were to ask me, I'd say I passed every test with flying colors. In the moment though, I felt as if I had failed, as if I wasn't good enough for the world, thus leading to my lack of interest in living. Nobody likes losing. Nobody wants to be a loser. No one wants to feel irrelevant or inadequate so that allows those thoughts to ponder and fester until the point you reach your proverbial breaking point. Unfortunately, some people break. Fortunately for others, like myself, we bend, not break. Instead, we gain confidence, as well as perspective. So no, this isn't about me succumbing to the pressures and fears of failure. This is about the euphoric self-realization that life is fickle and flimsy while death is definite. And, speaking logically, shouldn't you always invest in the constant, the guaranteed? Jesus and I both share the name "Emmanuel," so it's not too far-fetched to think that I can come back from the dead, as he did, but I'm not banking on that. I'm brokering that when I die, it's going to be meaningful. I've dedicated my whole life to dying.

"...let me tell you why I'm this way, hold on..."

-Shawn Corey Carter

CHAPTER

I

Take Off

"Emmanuel, so tell me how you feeling about this. You're going out into the world, all by yourself, nowhere to go, no place to live, but you do have a round trip ticket..." Mo said.

As she spoke, I just sat there, thinking to myself:

"Wow, I'm REALLY about to do this."

After careful consideration, I made it up in my mind that I wanted to do something different. That I wanted to shake the fruits from the tree. That I wanted to fly. That I wanted to soar. That I wanted to sail to the edge of the world and see if I'd fall off. I wanted to experience life on a different scale. I wanted to experience life under the most arduous conditions. I wanted to experience a life that I know I'd never succumb to. I wanted to experience a life that is an unfortunate yet everyday reality for everyday people. At one point or another, we all search for that life purpose and ponder:

"Is this how life is meant to be?"

That, among other questions, were those that I posed to myself consistently when approaching my 26th birthday. Just for clarity, I'm not one of those people who always thinks I'm right; I'm just never wrong. In the rare times, well, in the three times in life I've been wrong,

I've been the second to admit it. My three times in life of being wrong are as follows: As an 18 year old, I just knew that in life I'd be married by 22 with two kids. At the very least by the age of 26, I'd be a successful actor living in a mansion with money never being a problem. To my surprise, boy was I wrong. Those two dreams never manifested. Neither have my expectations of marrying Halle Berry and Nia Long. Such is life though, right?. So there I was, at the age of 25, single with zero kids, no mansion, and no waking up to Halle cooking me breakfast while me and Nia cuddled in bed watching *Coming 2 Americuh*. In reality, I was a part-time cashier crashing on my sister's couch watching *Monster's Ball*, metaphorically thinking to myself that this current role in life didn't fit me.

"Where did I go wrong?"

Like seriously, at what junction in life did I make the wrong decisions? Then, what I like to consider "optimismal wisdom" kicked in. Maybe I never went wrong. Maybe, at that point in life, that was where I was supposed to be. Only in hindsight can I look back now, at the age of 31, and say to myself that everything went according to plan. What I learned is that we have minimal control over our lives and for as long as we live, things will happen without our permission and without a moment's notice. It's not too far-fetched that as you're reading this you've flashbacked to your youth and remembered all the things you wanted and expected, only to realize that those things never came to fruition. Once I realized my life wasn't anything like I expected, I wanted to do something else unexpected. Something different. Something out of the box. Something I felt would bring me perspective and hopefully bring me some sort of consolation as well as a sense of self-worth and inner peace. Something like backpacking through Europe. Something like moving to a deserted island and living off the land. Something like winning the lottery. Something like finding out I'm adopted and that my birth parents were wealthy billionaires who had set up a trust fund for me that I could reclaim on my 26th birthday. Those options never materialized unfortunately so I had to find things within my budget to do. One day, while sitting atop my thinking seat, my brainstorming led me down a path of doing something that literally takes no money to do.

Be homeless.

Growing up, even through my adolescence and adulthood, I've always had a weird interest and fascination in the lives of homeless people. For instance, I remember how we'd always see the same guy outside McDowell's and how he'd always ask my dad for money and my dad would give him change. Other places we went we'd see other men and women who would ask my parents for change or food.

Why were those people out there?

What life transgressions led them to a life where they slept outside, dressed as they dressed, picked through garbage and asked for change?

In a moment of thought and reflection around the time of January-February-ish 2010-ish, I said, since I haven't experienced what I had expected to experience by that current age that I would go on a pilgrimage of sorts. A journey to learn more about myself. A journey to grow. A journey to gain more understanding on life as well as put my strength, resilience, and faith to the test. So I made up my mind that I would give up everything, go to a place I've never been and just live there...

...On the streets.

Now came the next decision of determining when I would do it.

One of the most important days in contemporary and cultural history occurred on April 2nd, 1984. It was on this day, at the University of Louisville Hospital in Louisville, KY, that arguably the most important birth, next to the birth of Jesus, occurred. Emmanuel Daniel Clack arrived into the world at 11:59pm weighing a whopping 10 lb 1oz. I honestly don't remember that day and most of you don't either but that's besides the point. The thing that we need to remember is that on that day, the hands typing these words, that you're currently mesmerized by, entered into the world. You're welcome. Since that magical and majestic day, my birthday has always been a celebrated event, within the realms of my own mind. It's something I really enjoyed and felt great about. It was something special to me. Growing up in a house where first of the month checks were all the craze, having a birthday around that time was extremely beneficial to me, more so than all my other siblings, especially my little sister Lydia. When her birthday came 21 days later, on April 23rd, it was more so an afterthought. She humorously, to this day, recalls how her birthdays always sucked because our parents invested more time, money and energy into mine. Rightfully so, if you ask me. It'd be noble of me to say I feel guilty or even had a shred of sympathy for her, but I don't. I'm not in charge of when government-issued checks are disbursed, but I was glad they decided to do so the day before my birthday because payday brings out the best in all of us. Right?

My parents spared no expense. I always had the best birthdays, from cookouts to pizza parties, always had the biggest cake, the most ice cream, the best gifts, etc etc. That rich tradition labored into my adult years.I have tried to always do something significant or meaningful around the time of my birthday. I got my first tattoo for my 18th birthday. For my 22nd, I got my second tattoo and TT and I threw myself a surprise birthday party that no one showed up for. Can you imagine that? Having a birthday party and literally no one shows up? I invited people, but nobody came. It was just me and her. For year 24, I decided to stay up for the entire 24 hours. Then came my 26th birthday, That year, I decided I'd up the ante and partake in this journey of faith, sacrifice and ambition to the great wild, wild west of Los Angeles, CA. Since I was turning 26, I felt it fitting to culminate my birthday by spending 26 days there. Not in a nice hotel or resort. Not at a friend's house. Not with a relative. Not even with so much as having a plan. Nope. Just go there and see what happens. This was going to be a trial and error pilgrimage that I mentally prepared for and said no matter what happens, always make the most of it, find the silver lining and just have a sense of humor about it.

The days leading up to my trip I purchased all the necessities, including one of those 12x12x21 camping backpacks from Wally World. It was big, but not too big (THAT'S WHAT SHE SAID!). I just wanted something to be able to store a week's worth of clothes as well as snacks and other things I'd need like toothpaste, toothbrush, lotion, liquid soap, deodorant and all that good stuff. The hard part was when it was time to pack. This was the Genesis of me conforming into what I eventually would become.

My goal was to pack 7 days-worth of clothes. 7 days of clothes didn't fit.

Next goal.

6 days worth of clothes. 6 days didn't work.

Next goal.

5 days worth of clothes.

5 days worked but I had 0 extra room left in my bag that I'd need in the event that I accumulated other stuff.

Next goal.

4 days worth of clothes.

FINALLY!

Four days was a good balance and it's the number that represents the month I was born in so I felt good about those odds.

One thing with compromise is that you get creative just based on the need of necessity. To help rationalize my choices I calculated that I only needed one pair of jeans, one pair of khaki pants and two pairs of basketball shorts, and a few pairs of socks. I packed three additional pairs of b-ball shorts that I wore as underwear since I didn't wear regular underwear and haven't since I was in high school, where during a moment of getting Freshman-hazed before basketball practice, my boxer shorts ripped and I had to go the rest of the day not wearing underwear. Needless to say, that trend has stuck with me from that moment until present day.

With limited clothing options, I would just depend on having to wash clothes every 4-5 days. In college, I used to wash clothes every two to three weeks and could legitimately go a month without washing clothes. My old apartment had a color coordinated walk in closet equipped with stacks of shoe boxes that contained shoes I may have had worn only once or twice. Some boxes contained shoes I had not even worn yet because I was waiting for a special event to break them out. These were things that I was very proud of. These were the times when I used to have my clothes dry cleaned. These are the times I would iron all my clothes and hang them up neatly so that my pants crease never lost their integrity. I departed from that luxury to know the compromise of having to fold pants four times over just so I could stuff them into my backpack.

It's often that I take real-life situations and turn them into life metaphors or try to find the message and purpose in why I'm doing something or why certain things happened. Packing that backpack was that initial realization that options are luxuries. I was stripping myself of luxuries, only allowing myself the necessities. It proved to be more revealing than I could have ever envisioned at that point. Five years later and I'm still folding pants four times over just so that I can stuff them into my backpack. Gone is the walk-in closet. Gone are the shoe boxes of shoes I've never worn. I travel with two pairs of shoes. Shoes that I wear every day. My walk in closet became walking" closet, which is a backpack that I carry all the time. It fits almost everything that I possess inside of it, minus a few pair of shoes and clothes that I keep at my parent's house in Kentucky.

In 2012, my grandmother passed, God rest her soul, LOVE YOU NANNY!!! While driving to her burial plot. Somebody brought up the fact within the context of conversation that "...You never see a U-haul behind a hearse..." as to say that when we die, we literally take nothing with us. So there I was, in 2010, going through that realization. Within that trip, I learned that nothing is for sure or for certain and that as long as your needs are covered, you'll never miss your wants because those are simply luxuries. Luxuries that many people aren't afforded. In third world countries. The things we discard or take for granted are the things they'd be excited to have. Coming from a person who literally dug through the trash hoping to find something to quiet the stomach rumbles, you learn a lot when you least expect it. Sometimes the best plan is never having one.

Once I got to LA, I abandoned my plans to wash clothes 4-5 days. It got to a point where I just wore the same thing 2-3 days in a row. The only thing I changed were my socks and the shorts I wore as underwear. As long as my clothes didn't smell, I'd wear them again. There wasn't anybody to say "Hey! You had that on yesterday!" There was no perception to guard against. Here I was, albeit in an unconventional way, beginning to find a form of freedom. Think about it, if you wear an outfit for a few hours and don't do any activities, then is it "dirty"? It's not "dirty," but it's just taboo to repeat outfits. The amount of shame to my game came to a grand total of $0.00. I'll wear the same pants every day so long as they don't smell. People wear jackets all day every day, back to back to back and it's not looked at as taboo to wear the same shoes every day, but with other clothing it is. Why?

Stigmas became something that I noticed while out in LA that really served no real purpose other than to, in a way, be used to belittle others and create division among individuals. The fear of not being yourself shouldn't be compromised, but, in society, it often is because some decisions come with ridicule. The car you drive, the house you live in, the job you have, the clothes you wear and even who you decide to love, is all subject to these superficial standards. They prevent people from being true to themselves or even developing into who they are or want to be.

This experiment showed me who I was on a much deeper level and allowed me to see the world differently. It was the kickstart for me to not allow myself to succumb to these standards and say to heck with ridicule. Personal happiness means more to me than opinions. We all have flaws but flaws are actually subjective. I decided to embrace my flaws and the truth that comes with them. It's turned me into a super version of myself and I must say that I'm the happiest I've ever been in my life. It's a powerful thing to not be fearful. To not be overly influenced by the opinions of others. To exhibit my fearless demeanor, I'll share with you all some personal details about myself that are sure to make you judge me, so grab your robe and gavel. There are some days that don't warrant a shower: if I'm sitting in the library all day, why take a shower? In LA, I went days without taking a shower and I still go a day without showering from time to time. If I'm just sitting around all day not doing anything then why waste water? There's a ton of people who don't shower every single day and have missed days here and there but it's too socially unappealing to mention or for them to even admit. Want to hear something real crazy? When I was a teenager I used to never brush my teeth. Well, ok, not never, but once every blue moon, definitely not daily. Back then, I just hated it for some reason. I don't know why. When I was 15-ish I remember going like a year without ever brushing my teeth. It wasn't until I went to the dentist, in an attempt to get braces, that I realized that I had a problem. The dentist asked how often I brushed my teeth, my reply was "everyday," but he wasn't fooled. I thought if I just wiped the plaque off of my teeth and chewed some gum then he'd never suspect a thing. To my chagrin, he wasn't fooled and because of that, I was denied braces. He told me that he didn't trust that I would take care of them by properly brushing my teeth. Since then, I brush almost every day... sometimes. In fact, there are days, I'll skip taking a shower but still brush my teeth. That feeling of having clean teeth just makes me feel great about myself, so much so, that I invest in buying the expensive toothpaste now: it's $5 bucks a tube baby. Before seeing the error of my ways, I used to buy whatever was on sale, but I take pride in that plaque-free feeling when I lick the front of my teeth. Oh, let me go back, my old version of "brushing my teeth" was using a wet rag and wiping across the front of my teeth.

Anyways, back to my point, wait, what was my point??

Oh, the concept of luxury and necessity.

In the years since LA, I've maintained my level of bare necessity: everything I have fits into a backpack. Gone is that walk-in closet color-coded to perfection. Now I shop at the Goodwill and buy the things I need at that time. In LA, my backpack was my house, my closet, my pillow, my pantry and my home gym. I adapted to that and it's stuck with me ever since. I'll get more in depth into this story as I go on but once you realize how amazing time and freedom feel you gravitate to maintaining that level of time and freedom. If you have a lot of stuff, you have to worry about keeping up with it all and moving it if you move. I'm travel-ready at all times, so I travel all the time.

There was a movie with George Blooney that I watched the other day, I can't remember the name of it, but in the movie he was a something, I honestly forgot. Aside from his job, which he had to travel routinely for, he was like a public speaker. Part of his speech, for which he'd hold seminars for a room of people, he would walk out in front of the people in attendance and sit an empty backpack on a table and ask somebody what they would put in their backpack. Wait, no, that's a lie. He asked them to picture their house and put it in the backpack, then their car, their kids and so forth and so on. In this fictional imaging, he told them to now try to put that backpack on. As you can imagine, you can't physically fit those things into one backpack and if you could, it'd be too heavy and impossible to carry. For the purpose of metaphors and drawing parallels, it was something that I obviously identified with. I understood the purpose of that mental regimen. His message was the concept of luxury versus necessity. I think. Well, close enough. Think about the things you NEED and the things you WANT. They are night and day. The only thing we NEED is water to live. In poverty stricken countries, they don't wear clothes or even shoes and don't live in houses so a lot of our "NEEDS" are WANTS that have filtrated through society to be made to be things that we need.

To quote a popular rap song from my teenage years:

> "Nobody need nobody, all I need is me and my dogs n*ℓℓa so f*ck all of y'all n*ℓℓas"

Which, in hindsight, is a bad example because he said he doesn't need nobody then names at least two bodies.

I'm going to leave it in because I like that song and it's what popped in my head when I was typing the sentence that preceded it.

Ok, next song:

No other songs are coming to me to go with my theory other than:

> "All by myself, don't wanna be by myself"

And that doesn't support my thoughts.

Oh, I know, I'll just make up a song:

> *"At the end of the day, all I have is me, at the end of the day, that's all I need"*

BOOYAH (Stewart Scott voice)

That. Just. Happened. (Wilt Ferrell voice)

If you were in this Stardollars on November 5th, 2015 at 3:22pm PST then just know you were in the presence of me freestyling this entire chapter.
I'm writing this on my laptop and you should see all the red lines to signal my spelling and grammatical errors, but because I'm just writing as it comes to me I don't have time to go back and edit I'm trying to stay in my zone. Feel me? But, I digress.

> *"At the end of the day, all I have is me, at the end of the day, that's all I need"*

The final inventory of my backpack, once I rationalized my needs and wants, were 1 pair of jeans, 1 pair of jogging packs, 1 jacket, 1 pair of khaki shorts, 4 pairs of socks, 3 t-shirts, 1 hoody, 4 pairs of basketball shorts, and 2 pairs of sneakers.

Let me ask you, if you were going on a trip for 26 days, what would you pack?

It doesn't have to only fit into a backpack but as you read this, think of what all you would pack, the number of suitcase you would take. To help you better envision things, it's the summer time so keep thinking of the items you'd pack for your 26 day trip. Now that you've packed. Take the number of suitcases you have and imagine catching a plane. How many bags do you check? How many do you take onboard?

You've landed, you've got your bags from baggage claim, now think how you're going to get your bags to where it is you're staying. Do you call a cab? Take a shuttle? Have a friend pick you up?

Now you have your bags and you've found a way to get to where you're going.

Once you get to where you're going, you can drop your bags off and relax right?

Correct me if I'm wrong, but I'm guessing all those thoughts were heavily based on you taking what you WANTED to take and not having to take only what you NEEDED.

New scenario:

Now imagine if you only packed ONE backpack to travel 25000 miles from where you're from to a place you've never been without anybody you know there, didn't check a bag, but took it onboard with you. When you landed, you exited the plane, walked through the airport, turned your camera on and just started walking...

...with no clue of where you're going...

...how you were going to get there...

...That's what I did.

Location: Atlanta, GA
Date: April 4, 2010

"Emmanuel, so tell me how you feeling about this, you're going out into the world, all by yourself, nowhere to go, no place to live, but you do have a round trip ticket... you can always come back home" Mo said.

If there was a bright side, it was that this is just temporary and, no matter what, I can always come home. Her words brought a sense of comfort into my frantic mind, as I sat there, not doubting myself, but questioning myself and just trying to grasp onto any optimism I could grab onto.

"So how do you feel, are you nervous?" she asked

"Ummm, I'm numb" I replied.

Really, I didn't know what to say, I had sooo many thoughts and scenarios running through my head.

"What are you going to do when you first get off the plane?" she proceeded to ask next.

"Ummm, I don't know" after taking a pause I said "Get off the plane" with a slight smirk.

I had no clue or inkling of what I was going to do or how I was going to feel.

She continued to pick my brain:

"And then where are you going to go?" she asked.

"Walking, to try to get outside" I replied.

These were the best answers I could provide. I was in the conversation, but really I wasn't involved in the conversation. As we sat on the couch in her apartment, I found myself in some sort of trance.The world almost stood still. It felt as if I was just in an altered state that could be best described as a concoction of fear, uncertainty, and confused anxiety. Knowing my pension for sarcasm, Mo just laughed at my last reply and offered her own insight:

>"I'm pretty sure you get on the highway, I mean like get on a shuttle or something, I'm the sure the airplane, I mean the airport isn't in the city" she said.

>"Yeah, you're right" I replied.

>"Don't take a taxi" she said with a light laugh.

It's my guess that she was realizing just how ill-prepared I was just from my responses or lack thereof.

>"I didn't think about that" I replied.

>"You need me to go with you?" she jokingly offered.

>"It can't be that far" I said.

>"Think about the Atlanta airport and the city, can't walk" she quickly quipped.

>"Do they have buses?" I asked.

>"I've never been to LA in my life" she replied.

>"I just know when we went to New York, we flew into Jersey and they had buses that took us, that would take you to New York" I pointed out.

Well, I hope they had buses. I never even thought about that. It's like I ignored all the minor details and focused more about where I would sleep, what I would do, and all the other dangers or situations I'd potentially face. Clearly in my haste, I neglected to put the horse before the wagon and simply just map out how to even get from the airport to downtown.

"I'm sure LA does too, but you might want to look and see what's the cheapest route" she added.

"That's what I'm banking on, so if worst comes to worse I'll just go stay with Kobe, me and him are cool" I replied

"Ron Artest seems a little more down to earth" she said.

"Ron Artest is probably gay" I retorted.

"Even better" she quickly replied.

That elicited a quick chuckle and smile from me and a much needed break from the angst that had begun to mount. Mo got me, she understood me. I was grateful for her at this point in my life. Although none of my fears had subsided fully, I felt a sense of calm after our quick talk.

"Well, enjoy" Mo said while preparing to turn off the camera, I turned my head, smiled and just waved.

Mo never fully voiced her concerns and apprehension of me leaving, even tho I could tell she had the same fears. We continued to talk the rest of that night just about the situation and the dynamic of our relationship while I'm in LA and when I come back. To be honest, I didn't want to leave her, we had a great thing going. We met and it was like a generic form of love-at-first sight, we just really enjoyed each other's company and, before we knew it, we shared each other's company every day. We used to joke about how I came over for the first time and never left. It was just at this moment in time, I had to leave, not because I wanted to, but I just felt like it was something I HAD to do.

The next morning when I woke up, I double checked everything making sure I had everything, then just loafed around the apartment. In my loafing, I neglected to check my flight's departure time and thought it was later than it actually was. We ended up being late heading to the airport. Mo and I hurried to get ready and rushed to the airport. To be truthful, I'd say that 65% of me didn't want to leave and was hoping to miss my flight. I've never been a person to say one thing and do another or punk out so I went through with it, even though I felt uneasy about it. While in the car I looked out the passenger window and began to cry. One tear turned to two, then so forth and so on. Mo reached over and grabbed my hand as she drove. Through my crying, I muscled up the strength to look over to her and muffle the words "I don't want to leave you." I was beyond sad. I wasn't sure how things between me and her would be after I left. There were so many variables and unknowns. She had expressed that me leaving kind of felt like I would leave and, in a sense, never come back. Throughout our relationship, I remained apprehensive about "titles." We weren't "boyfriend and girlfriend", even though we acted as such. Don't ask me why, but I felt more comfortable in that setting than with the added pressure of having titles to live up to. She wanted that title, but understood that having me around and not having that title was a compromise that, for the time being, she was willing to live with. We both kind of knew and were sure it wasn't going to be the same once I got back. She didn't want me to leave and felt as if me leaving was because I didn't want to be there and didn't seriously have interest in pursuing a future between the two of us. It's too hard to know what you want and to maintain what you have. It's almost like, if you're happy here, then why leave? Why now? Those were the thoughts that Mo had. The thoughts that I had were that I just felt in my spirit and in my heart, my life meant something bigger. It's my personal belief that a higher power summoned me to be something at that time. What that something was? I didn't know, but when I decided to leave it was done so with the trust and belief that this was my calling.

The closer we got to the airport, the more we clinched to each other's hand, I was just thinking about how much I was going to miss her and how I was essentially leaving comfort for the unknown and it frightened me. What if I never saw her again? What if something really bad happen to her while I was gone? So many worries clouded my brain.

As I nerve-wracked my brain with these thoughts, I gripped her hand tightly, just looking at her, not speaking. Shaking my head as tears fell from my face. She began to cry. I reached over and wiped away her tears from her cheek then rubbed the back of her neck as I kissed her hand. Pulling up at the airport, I looked at all of the people going inside and briefly debated on if I wanted to follow suit or just call the whole thing off. Mo and I looked at each other in silence. Her eyes were so sad. Her face was just so innocent and precious. I could tell she just didn't know what to say or how to feel. We had developed a nice bond in our time together. Seeing the same face every morning and every night for six months was comforting to me. Cooking dinner together, doing laundry, coordinating things like what to pick up on the way home from work. What we would do on the weekends. Going to the gym together. Watching SVU marathons and DVDs together. Meeting up for lunch. I was going to miss that routine of always having somebody else to consider when making decisions. Regardless of my lacking verbal acknowledgment of commitment, I was committed to her. While stalling to get out of the car, I just looked at her and said to myself:

"Damn she's so beautiful, I can't leave her"

As much as I didn't want to, like I said, I knew I had a destiny to fulfill and a purpose to pursue. We exited the car, she walked around to my side, stepped on the curb and as we exchanged a long deep hug and kiss. We held each other tightly, not wanting to let go. Finally, after what didn't feel like a long enough goodbye, I grabbed my backpack flung it around my shoulders and proceeded to walk into the airport while momentarily looking back to see her car pull away from the curb and honk at me.

Once inside, I made it through security matriculating my way through Hartsfield-Jackson airport while ducking and dodging through crowds of people, running through the airport with my hands holding my backpack straps as I sprinted past people, stopping on a dime to change direction, even at one point utilizing a well timed spin move to evade a would be defender; well a rolling luggage that a person was toting behind them but same difference. Had I been a few minutes later, or not the incredible athlete that I am, I would have missed my flight because, as I approached my gate, I heard my name over the intercom.

CHAPTER
II

Cotton

Time is the greatest luxury and commodity in life, if you ask me. It's the one thing you can never get back. When I told others of how I spent 26 days living on the streets, plenty of people asked:

"Why?"

And the answer is simple.

I didn't do it. Destiny did. I was physically present during the entire ordeal but it was a spiritual journey. The life journey before I got to the point of deciding to take this spiritual journey is a story that is layered and full of pain, anger, angst, doubt, fear, confusion and abandonment. But hold on, let me tell you why I'm this way.

Location: Bowling Green, KY
Date: February IDK, 2008

"What's the count?" I demanded.

"11-11" somebody replied.

Like many other collegiate students, many of my hours, sweat and blood were spent on the recreational basketball courts inside of the Preston Center on the campus of Western Kentucky University. It was the epicenter for failed, misguided, derailed hoop dreams, as well as a sanctuary for competition. In this place, disputes over fouls led to fist fights and game winning shots gave you that feeling of March Madness with full-out celebratory sprints onto the court and huddles of jubilation. In this place, dreams of hitting clutch, game-winning or game-tying shots manifested. In this place, the most unlikely of shots found the bottom of the goal; posters get made; ankles get broken; trash gets talked and threats are promised and upheld. This is the place we called home. We spent day in and day out in this place. Winning mattered: this was a war zone. This wasn't your country club friendly contest. These were battles. These were my golden years. There were no nets being cut down here. There were no trophies. There were no medals. There were no awards. There was only pride to play for. Games were played to 12 and with the game tied at 11-11, like the one I found myself in, it was clutch time for elite athletes to seize the moment, dig deep and rise above any obstacles in their way and snatch victory from the grasp of your opposition's cold dead hands. These were the moments when the brightest stars shined. In these moments, I did what I do:

SHINE.

To help capture the ambiance of the following event of epic proportions, it's probably best to read the forthcoming passage in slow motion:

There I was, in a textbook defensive stance keeping watch over whoever I was guarding. I won't even try to remember who the other team was, but for the sake of this story, we'll just refer to them as suckas and jive turkeys. One of the aforementioned suckas is dribbling at the top of the key, he passes it to some other jive turkey on the wing. This is one of those guys who watched one too many And 2 mixtapes growing up and clearly wanted to play hero ball. I cheated my way to provide help defense if by chance he was able to elude his defender and get open. He dribbled around a few times in an attempt to get to the rim then used a step back move to create space and then released a high-arching jumper. As he released the ball, I could tell that he was going to miss. I just have that instinct to know these things. I immediately turned and prepared to go in for the rebound. I was on the opposite side of the court so I had a nice vantage point of how the rebound would come off the rim, based on the trajectory of the ball, it was going to bounce high off the front of the rim. Don't ask me how I know, it's just a thing you pick up from playing when you can tell if a shot is going to be short and miss the rim or if it's going to go in. I can't provide any science or analytics to explain why, this isn't Sports Science, which by the way, I LOVE to watch. It's super amazing to me how they can create quantitative results and measure everything about a person. Iit's the things we'd never even think to factor into why a person is good but they provide scientific results to show how dominant athletes are so dominant. But, I digress.

Rolling to the paint, I'm fixated on the ball, it made contact with the rim and bounced off the rim and high into the sky. Soaring in like a falcon; out-jumping everybody around me. I corralled the ball with my right hand, then, with my left hand, emphatically slapped the ball between my hands. As I landed, I immediately took off dribbling while taking a quick gander up court. Due to the fact that the rebound came to the middle of the paint, I had a decisive head start on half of their team. There were only two helpless suckas ahead of me retreating back on defense. In a mad dash, I raced down the court to do what I've done countless times before on that very court;

GET BUCKETS!

Before there was Lebron, there was "Clack" True story, in 2003, one of Lebron's high school games came on ESPN and the next day in the gym somebody comes up and tells me about this high school kid who plays like me. My basketball style of play was aggressive, a physically imposing player who adored contact and would go out of my way to lower my shoulder into defenders on my way to the rim and still have the balance, finesse and body control to make the layup. Speaking as humbly as I can, I was virtually a one man fast break. I don't need Sports Science for this, just ask my peers and they'll corroborate it. I was a 6'3 205 pound freight train coming at you full speed. Full steam ahead. As I'm chugging up the court like a locomotive, I survey the defense and I know If I can split the two of them I can get to the rim. Thanks to the fact I take long strides, I only needed to get one step past the 3 point line before taking two steps then taking flight towards the rim. In a split second, I had passed half court. One dribble. Two dribbles. At this point, the two defenders had broken down in a defensive stance in a desperate and somewhat laughable attempt to keep me from scoring. Laughing My Arse Off. By this time, I was one step inside the 3 point line and cleared for take off. I faked a crossover to the right just to create space to slash between them; I took one step...

Next step...

SNAP!

As I crashed to the court, I knew something was horribly wrong. I closed my eyes tightly in an attempt to shut out the pain. While my eyes were closed, I saw a bright light, then my life began to flash before my eyes. Instantly, I was 7 years old again, playing basketball at the local elementary school with my parents cheering in the stands. That morphed into me being in 9th grade and in the gym after school attempting to dunk unsuccessfully numerous times until that moment when I finally managed to dunk for the first time. That faded into that one time I beat Michael Jordan in a game of 1 on 1 and he told me, "You're going to be the greatest player of all-time. I'm envious of your talents". It should be noted that only 2 of those aforementioned things occurred in real life. But I digress. As I layed there, I heard a voice ask me "Are you ok?" I replied, "God, is that you!?" I opened my eyes to look around and see what heaven looked like. Immediately, I reached for my ankle just to make sure it was still attached to my body. After confirming it was still there, I just laid there on my back contemplating life; thinking to myself that at this junction in my life had I done enough to make my mom proud? Did I take my clothes out the washer and put them in the dryer this morning? and why do they always bring the McRib back?

Flashback with me for a quick second if you don't mind. The worst pain I've EVER felt was when I had fractured my finger while playing basketball in Preston Center almost 5 years prior to this injury. Just so we can create a nice dialogue amongst us, let me preface everything I say from hereafter with an understanding that I'm not the best when it comes to doing things in a timely manner. I'm a habitual procrastinator and I put things off all the time. That said, It was one month after fracturing my finger before I even went to the doctor. The sad part is that it wasn't my idea to go. I actually never planned to go but my dad kept harassing me about it and basically forced me to go. Due to the extent of the injury, I needed to have surgery which required having small metal pins inserted into my finger to help set the bone so that it could heal properly. Let me tell you about that lovely experience and the fortune of having the pleasure of those metal pins that they had placed in my finger literally YANKED out without any anesthesia or numbing agent.

It was a brisk spring day in 2003, I journeyed down to Norton's Hospital in Louisville, KY with my dad. He dropped me off and instructed me to call him when I was done. I was 19, so I didn't need anybody to go with me. I was a big boy now. I had chest hairs and everything. Besides, I figured it'd be a nice simple quick "in and out" procedure as the nurse on the phone explained to me when I made my appointment. What I've learned in life is that the truth is a touchy subject. Had she had said "Sir, just to be honest with you, this is going to be the worst pain you've ever experienced..." then it's highly likely that I may not have agreed to these terms. To her credit, maybe it is a simple procedure on most days. Unfortunately, I picked the wrong day. Just imagine sitting at a table and having somebody with a pair of pliers pull pins out of your finger. If that's not bad enough, have that same somebody use your procedure as a teaching tool and have four observers also in the room. It's a common notion that you can't talk and listen at the same time. One notion I swiftly realized is that you can't take pins out of a person's finger and engage a room of onlookers at the same time either. Due to the fact that the doctor was talking, he wasn't fully engaged into the procedure and as he went to pull a pin out with the pair of pliers, he repeatedly missed while trying to clamp onto the end of the pin and therefore pinched my skin every time. Once he clamped onto a pin it wasn't like the pin just slid right out. He had to pull on it harder to get it out. This all occurred for 15-20 minutes. Just rethinking about that makes me cringe.Time has passed since then, but I've always maintained that if I ever saw that doctor on the street then it'd be on like Donkey Kong. Believe you me!

All things considered, the pain I felt in my ankle on that fateful day in Preston was only second to that debauchery at the hands of Dr. Douche Bag. If I may just install a footnote about this day, aside from my ankle being messed up, at the moment, I was more upset that I MISSED the layup. That would have made matters a little more bearable had I at least made the shot. As you can imagine, I didn't physically see what happened to my ankle but onlookers described the scene and told me that when I stepped my foot rolled to the side and my ankle bent in half and that the outer ankle part touched the court. Most injuries wouldn't occur like that and maybe their ankle wouldn't have completely bent over but that's just me, I have a flair for going above and beyond and setting new precedence in the things I do. It's like I always tell my nephew. "If you're going to do something, be good at it".

After sitting on the ground for like 20 minutes, I was able to get help standing up and hobbled my way to the couches at the entrance of the gym. Several people walked over to check on me and share their condolences. It wasn't verbally said, but I could tell it was heartbreaking to see such a beloved figure hurt and that the gym wouldn't be the same without me. A few of the staffers worried of the ramifications of me no longer being able to play and how it would affect people's desire to come in there and play basketball. It was like everybody's hopes were dashed and dreams deferred. If I'm not there then seriously why would anybody come in there? Right? Jk. Seeing the concern in the eyes of my peers and feeling the moral be sucked out of the building, I put on a good face and assured them I was ok. I honestly felt ok and just thought it was a really bad ankle sprain. In my mind, I diagnosed that I'd miss a couple days on the courts then be ready to get back to what I do best:

GET BUCKETS!

All those thoughts changed as soon as I stood up. I'm not sure how to type the sound I made at this point but it's something of a high pitched screech. Something of the falsetto variety mixed with the sound one would make if somebody poured ice cold water on you unexpectedly. It was a concoction of shock and discomfort all combined into an auditory reply. It wasn't in the least bit a manly noise, I'll just say that.

I'm confident and secure enough in my manhood to share that with you. When I say that ish HURT, chile, listen here hunny, that thing HURTED!!! I could put literally no weight on my ankle. Zero. Zilch. Nona. Nada. Again, this is what set me apart from others, a normal person in that moment would seek immediate medical attention. Did I? Nope. Not me. Instead, I Kunta Kinte'd my way to Jimmy's car and had him drop me off at my apartment where I hopped up the stairs into my apartment and into my room. Once in my room, I took off my socks and shoes and was highly disturbed by what I saw. My ankle was swollen on both sides and looked BAD. (see Figure 1.1) The girl I was involved with at the time was there, she looked at it and, like many women, her maternal instincts kicked in and she made me go to the hospital. The diagnosis:

Fractured ankle.
Torn tendons.
Torn cartilage.
Ruptured Spleen.

Something had happened to my Achilles. I think they categorized it as a partial tear. The doctor informed me that I would have been better off breaking my ankle because the healing process for my ankle would have been easier. Unfortunately for me, I didn't have that luxury of breaking it. I was faced with having to use crutches for nearly two months, soaking my ankle in a tub of ice everyday, taking prescribed pain medicine and antibiotics. If I had health insurance I'm 100% they would have suggested that I have surgery. Since I didn't, they gave me the old heave heaux: the heal on your own and just hope for the best form of treatment.

And just like that:

Grand Opening.

Grand Closing.

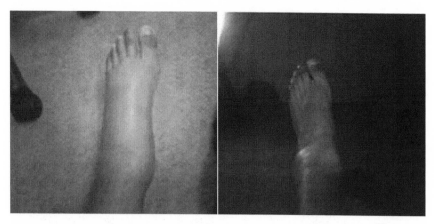

Figure 1.1

The term "too much time on your hands" is how I'd describe my healing process. The only thing is, I didn't ask for this time and didn't want this time. All I wanted was to be the same 5th year Junior that I had always been. The same 5th year Junior who would go to class sparingly; play basketball and eat free food from McDowell's. This was the turning point in my 31 years of existence. Some could refer to it as a "quarter life crisis." There was no real way of knowing how any of this would affect me but I'll explain as we go along. It's kind of ironic to me that one of the worst things that ever happened to me physically led to the best thing ever happening to me spiritually. Not sure of the source of the saying but there truly is "beauty in the struggle" and this was the genesis to my greatest struggle. This injury was the catalyst to the world as I knew it crashing down around me. From there my downward spiral began.

My life prior to me getting injured was pretty decent. I had a great thing going. Being 22, single, own car, own apartment, part time job at McDowell's and a full time job collecting 4k a semester in student loan residual checks. Not a bad life right? Unlike some of my peers, I was fiscally responsible. My money was spent wisely to pay my rent and my car note up to at least 3 and 2 months in advance respectfully. By my own standards, I had everything I needed and was comfortable. That comfort was replaced with constant discomfort. Sleeping with your foot propped up isn't as relaxing as it sounds. Especially when that ankle is constantly throbbing in pain. There's no comfort in having to crawl on your knees to the kitchen from your room and back because it's too hard to use crutches and hold food simultaneously. There's nothing comfortable about submerging your feet into tubs of ice every morning. The biggest lack of comfort is having to endure all of this, alone. There's no comfort in realizing that you're all by yourself.

It's a fair assessment to say that up to that junction in my life, the general consensus of my peers was that I was "popular " with no shortage of friends, acquaintances or love interests. I wasn't acclimated with being a reclusive person. I was acclimated with always being out and about for pretty much my entire life. There wasn't any idle time to be had. These were my golden year. I loved being in college, I loved that freedom, I loved being able to be responsible for myself and do all the things I enjoyed. I highly enjoyed hanging with my friends attending all the functions deploying our antics of parking lot pimping, and gyrating on members of the opposite sex. I even had a gyrating maneuver that I would bestow upon women during parties that came to be known as "The Clack" I won't share any details of the move in question because what happens in Garrett Hall stays in Garrett Hall. "Clack" is what everybody knew me as, referred to me as and would yell from across the campus, across the dining hall and wherever they saw me. This was life to me, this is what I thrived on and in an instant my life changed and I was severely ill-advised on how to adapt to that change.

On those days being secluded in the room by my myself there wasn't anybody yelling my name from across the kitchen or from across the living room. The only yells were my yells of frustration;

"URRRRGGGGHHHH"

My yells of pain.

"FFFFUUUGGGHH!!!!!!!!!!!!!!!!!!!!!!!"

It was a constant discomfort. I've never been a medication person because I've always felt like it was a placebo. It doesn't actually heal you, it just gives you psychological comfort. You're not going to stay sick forever so taking meds really isn't curing things that will heal naturally without anything. This time was different. I wasn't sick. I was in pain. I need to psychologically mask it all. I over indulged on pain pills, the more I took the more I felt that I needed. The more that I felt I needed the more I wanted them. Heck, I just wanted anything but to be in this position.

As the months rolled by, I eventually stopped watching TV in exchange of just laying in my bed and staring at the wall. The aforementioned girl I was involved at the time of my injury betrayed my trust and at my suggestion packed up her things and left. What I began to notice was that everything gets magnified once you have time to think and analyze situations. There was an instance in which she had told me of her whereabouts one night and at the time I believed it. Later on once I found out she had lied, I didn't hold it against her. I've never been a person to question other people too in depth. I was preoccupied with just living life. Idle time creates an active mind, so I started to take notice to who exactly this person I was sharing my space with and noticed a lot of character flaws. Flaws I overlooked. She's a very sweet, beautiful and lovely person so this isn't to try to throw her under the bus.There's nothing but love and respect for her. The situation that I found myself in dealing with a dishonest person was the reality that they're capable of doing anything. It's hard to trust that they're going to maintain being honest or revert to telling convenient truths in favor of hiding facts that will reflect negatively on them. A few months prior when made aware of her current living situation without hesitation I insisted that she come live with me because I wanted to help take her out such an unfortunate situation and take away some of the stress she was going through because I genuinely cared about her. It wasn't until later that I found out that she fabricated her living situation to merely gain my sympathy so that she could move in with me. Even still, once knowing the truth, I still let her stay. Flash forward to now not being able to drive and take her the places she needed to go, I became almost disposable. The lies continued until finally I was like it isn't worth it. Trust is hard to build but easy to lose.

As I laid in bed, I noticed how little activity my phone was receiving, I felt even more disposable and began to slowly lose trust in the things and people around me. Have you ever seen the movie "The Truman Show"? That is what I was experiencing. Everything around me was a facade. I was slowly starting to realize it and trying to piece together these fabrications.

Do these people really care about me?

Are these people really my friends?

As I laid in bed, I asked myself all of this and mentally went down the list of all the people I knew and realized how none of them, well not none but the vast majority of them didn't call to check up on me, stop by or anything. My primary pet peeve is lying. The worst thing you can do to me is LIE to me. The mind fornication for me at the age of 23 thinking my life was a complete lie was disturbing. It felt like a shallow realm of existence and the realization that the people around me weren't around me for genuine reasons startled me. Even if they were, I really couldn't trust that they were. While laying in my bed countless nights, I developed a new sense of paranoia. It felt as if everybody was against me. My defense mechanism was to be leery of everybody. There's no way of knowing who's for you or against you. My only remedy and logical solution was to group everybody as being against me and be surprised as to who's for me rather than to assume somebody is for me only to find out that they're actually against me. This was my reality, well the reality being confined in a solitary situation created. It wasn't long before I started to resent certain people. This led to me resenting even more people. My resentment extended to not only include people but to include the way people think and the way people act. Particularly the people in the world around me.

As I laid in my bed, My views on the world changed. I started to question just about any and everything, even finding time to question my own thoughts and beliefs.

Why am I a Christian?

Why did I come to college?

Why am I afraid of commitment?

What I distinguished in realizing the answers to those questions was that I was influenced by standards and by society. There was a rebellious energy that began to form within me. I began to reject everything. I didn't want to be of this world. Didn't want to exist in this world. Didn't want to even LIVE in this world.

As I laid in my bed, I looked back on all the times I was told of the things I couldn't or shouldn't do and how I listened.

As I laid in my bed, I thought about all the times I did things just to appease and make others happy.

As I laid in bed, I realized that my singular fear of death wasn't a fear anymore, It had become a wish of mine. It was dire that I get away from this facade that was built around me. I just wanted to be FREE.

This metamorphosis is what I'd like to perceive potentially occurred in "The Truman Show" after his boat hit the wall. Nobody knows what happened after he climbed that ladder. Nobody knows how that affected him long term. Want to know how it affected me? I began to desire isolation and find comfort in feeling uncomfortable. I found solace in being alone. They always say it's always the closest ones to you who hurt you. With nobody close to me I felt safe. I began to feel at peace. I began to allow my mind to expand. I began to think independently. I began to change. I began to evolve. I began to realize that it's up to me to love me. It's up to me to trust me. It's up to me to believe in me. It's up to me to always be there for me. It''s up to me to distance myself from things and people. I had to take control. I had to fight for what I wanted. I had to fight for my freedom. I had to fight for my peace. I had to fight for my happiness. About a month or so after my injury, I regained my ability to walk, albeit with a limp, but even with this new found mobility, I didn't use it to go outside often. Instead, I stayed in my apartment without any desire to be around people. I had climbed that ladder, climbing back down wasn't appeasing to me. Alas, on one evening in March, I climbed down.

One of the main selling points for me staying in college for as long as I did, aside from the refund checks, was intramural basketball. Intramural basketball was our playoffs. Daily pick up games was the regular season. Everything kicked up a notch during intramural season. Everybody positioned themselves throughout the regular season to assemble a team worthy of hoisting that trophy up at the end of the tournament. My college buddies forged ahead without me. I decided to suspend my weeks of self loathing and go out to support my guys. This was my first time returning to the Preston Center and for some odd reason I expected a shattering series of applause, yells and chants as soon as people realized I was in attendance. Do you all want to know what I got?

KICKED OUT!

Can you believe that I got KICKED OUT because I laughed during the national anthem?? Sure, it's not the most respectful or patriotic thing to do, however, ev-ery-bod-y was laughing and cracking smiles during it. The guy who they had selected to sing the anthem was a goof ball. He was always acting silly and clowning around. To see him dressed up and singing the anthem was completely unexpected, as well as, humorous to myself and several others. After the anthem concluded, one of the staffers at the Preston Center approached me and asked me to leave. Alimoe, who was a referee and friend of mine, happened to be standing next to the staffers during the anthem and had given me the heads up that they were coming for me. They came.

There's an unwritten common courtesy to not hit a man with glasses but I quickly realized that there weren't any unwritten common courtesies of how to treat a man on crutches dealing with depression and past suicidal demons. It's clearly fair game to ask said man to exit the facility and not care that his ride has yet to play a game so he'd have no way to even get home. Also to ignore the fact that he can't walk sufficiently enough to go anywhere else on campus in the meantime. All for laughing? This is what I left the comfort of my isolation for? To be singled out? To be embarrassed? My newfound rebel spirit was highly offended by this request and refused to leave. Why should I leave? Why should I allow myself to be unfairly treated? At this junction, the staffer requested the assistance of law enforcement officers who were already present. Once the law enforcement officers came over I spoke my peace and admitted to no wrongdoing and just left on my own terms when I felt ready to leave. It was important to stand my ground and speak my mind. To make claims to the officers of why I needed to be escorted off the premises, the staffer made reference to an isolated incident that occurred years prior when I allegedly made physical contact with a intramural referee and threatened to kill him. Due to those allegations I had been given a lifetime ban from participating in intramural sports. The incident in question was another situation poorly blown out of proportion to depict me as the bad guy. The insistence of mentioning that incident made me feel even more disgruntled. What the staffer failed to mention was that my actions were a reaction. Nobody just walks up to a person smacks his hand down and retorts with verbal aggression or the threat of murder for no reason. They always say that the truth derives from lies. Inaccuracies were painting me as a misfit, trouble maker but the facts weren't accurately presented. What was presented was a conventional truth to give the officers probable cause to form negative opinions about me. Never would I manipulate a situation to paint myself negatively. Never would I have an agenda and ulterior motive to get back at myself. Never would I not give myself the benefit of the doubt and instead make hasty decisions that weren't to my own benefit. So why is this person? Why have people in the past? What's going to stop people in the future from doing so?

Fresh off 4 weeks of isolation and seclusion and the first time I come back into society I get asked to vacate the facilities. To vacate a place I came to seek refuge. To vacate a place I dedicated so much time, effort and energy into. To vacate a place I loved to be. To vacate a place I expected to come back to and feel a taste of normalcy and take a break from the bubble I had blocked myself in. To come to a place that I expected to help me heal. Instead, I came to a place that had changed. To a place that no longer felt familiar. To a place I was no longer welcome. To a place where the joy that once existed was replaced with angst.

As I laid in my bed that night, I learned about my true self and how over the years I had developed a coping mechanism of using sarcasm and laughter to mask the deep underlying emotion that I kept buried away. Hitting that proverbial Truman Show wall with my boat helped me notice the lies in the world around me. It also allowed me to be aware of the lies within myself. These lies become toxic because I would suppress a lot of things and not talk about the things bothering me. My only remedy was playing basketball, writing or staying active. I'd take my basketball to whichever basketball court was around me and shoot around. It was a way to get away from the feeling of being down. The internal conflict that was mounting was that I'm not strong enough to suppress everything and that those days of feeling down weren't just days of feeling down, it was depression. Depression that I ignored. Depression that I never had to face head on because I kept myself busy. Within my isolation of never leaving my apartment I didn't have those distractions. All I had was the truth. All I had was the confrontation of deciphering between manipulated facades and reality. The reality was that I wasn't happy. Outside looking in, you'd never think the class clown, the guy who is always laughing and joking was the same guy who'd sit in a dark room and cry to himself.

The answers to my questions I previously presented began to unveil themselves. Slowly I realized things about my life up to that point. I realized that I never got over my breakup with my "first love". I realized I was to blame for my commitment issues. I realized how I built up an impermeable wall to keep others away. I realized that this wall was the reason I never let anyone in. It's the reason why a lot of my past relationships never flourished. There was a disconnect with my emotions. My emotions didn't exist beyond a certain point. I was guarded. I felt like giving a little of myself was too much to give. When giving your entire all to a person doesn't work out, you become lost. I was emotionally lost.

Defining my religion came next. I grew up in the church, we went three or four times a week. It was never an option, it was a for certain. It was something that we had to do, It was something we had to believe in. Something we couldn't go against or even question. It was instilled in us to have blind faith and trust in this omnipresent being and take everything said to you as law and as God's will or else be condemned to hell and labeled blasphemous. During this point in my life, I was beginning to feel like I was essentially losing everything. The first thing I lost was trust. The next thing I lost was faith. I lost faith in everything. To me it was more lies. I never had the option to decipher between what I put my faith in or didn't put my faith in. Over my life, I have met people from all walks of life with various backgrounds and religions and they were amazing people. Due to the fact these people weren't Christians, they're going to hell? That didn't seem reasonable to me. Let me backtrack. I didn't lose my spiritual faith, I lost my religious faith because that faith was man made. I began to try to rationalize my conflict with these beliefs laid out in front of me. Jesus nor God wrote the bible. Since I had lost trust in man why would I continue to put my faith into something man made and something that I can't prove did or didn't happen? Everything fell under the category of being a manipulated facade and I just stopped putting any energy, time, trust and faith into man. From here on I'd put all that energy, time, faith and trust into finding out who I was as a man.

"Born Alone, Live Alone, Die Alone"

Became my new found Mantra. It was a rebirth of sorts. It was the rebuilding of a person that I allowed to let previous life fallacies tear down. There were sentiments of regret, I felt foolish by letting my life be dictated by others. One of those regrets was the regret of having to quit basketball my senior year of High School even tho I really didn't want to but at that time it was the easier decision to make to just ignore the blatant disrespect I felt. Added to my list of regrets was attending Western Kentucky. My dream had been to attend the University Of Miami and get as far away from Kentucky as I could but I allowed the decision to be stifled by my relationship and do what I felt was right at the time.

As all of these thoughts and transformations began to transpire, I was forced to move back home to my parents house. I traded in the freedom of having freedom and opportunity for sleeping on the couch in the basement. Not being able to walk means not being able to work. Not being able to work means not being able to make money. Not being able to make money means not being able to pay rent. Not being able to pay rent means coming home to an eviction notice and avoiding calls from the leasing office. Due to the fact I withdrew from college that previous semester, I didn't have the luxury of those residual checks to rely on.

As I laid on the couch in the basement, I began to resent myself. I began to question why I'm even alive. I began to contemplate about taking my life. Much like countless other individuals who have suffered in silence, suicide wasn't foreign to me. It was something I had tried previously in life. Obviously to no avail. The initial attempt occurred around the time I was 19-ish. The reason behind that was mainly just out of immaturity and anger because the girl I loved moved on and I didn't. On the news, I used to always hear stories about people who took a bunch of pills during suicide attempts. One day I reached that breaking point. I was home alone just floating around at my parents house. While walking past the kitchen I noticed a half bottle of pills on the counter. I grabbed the bottle and took 4 at a time until the bottle was empty. One thing I never took into consideration was the type of pills these people used in their attempts. I assumed any pills would do the trick. Being a novice at suicide attempts, I didn't know that taking aspirin wouldn't be enough to kill me. In fact, the only thing that happened is that I developed diarrhea. Too much information? I know. Sorry. That lackluster and ill advised attempt aside, There was an another attempt. This time I was a little more calculated because at the age of 21-ish I was more adversed to life and knew that surely that if I get in my car and go 80 miles per hour on the highway and let go of the wheel then I'd crash and surely die...

...hopefully.

This time I did everything right. I ventured down I-65 South, unbuckled my seatbelt, mashed the gas, got up to about 90 miles per hour then let go of the wheel and closed my eyes...

.....

Once I opened my eyes, I was in total shock! Not only was I not dead but my car was still on the highway. The alignment on my car wasn't balanced which caused my car to pull to the left. Conventional wisdom would suggest that me letting go of my steering wheel would cause the car to pull to the left per usual and careen into the ditch along the road. No such luck, the car kept going straight. As tears drenched my face I just grabbed the wheel, got off at the next rest stop and spent the night in my car. There's probably some religious perspective to add here and to say hey maybe it was divine intervention but nevertheless I came to the conclusion that killing myself wasn't something that I was good at.

Those times of suicide were based strictly out of not getting my way or feeling like I was inadequate. This time was different, I just didn't want to exist in a world where money means more to people than being helpful to others. In a world where the truth is never told and lies and propaganda dictate our every move. My desire to escape grew more intense. I physically didn't want to harm myself but in effect I did want to just give up on life. I gave up on being a part of society. I gave up on trying to fit in. I gave up on accepting what I'm told. I gave up on being controlled. There's so much conspiracy and conflict in our society with no real common cause or reason.

As I laid on the couch in the basement I asked:

Is there really not a cure for cancer or aids?

Why is Black History only taught once a year?

Why is Christmas supposed to be about Jesus yet Santa Claus is more prevalent?

Slowly the answers began to present themselves to me, well, what I believe might be the answers. What I deduced is that there are systematic occurrences from history that are used in order to control people. Fear is implanted into the minds of everybody to make you feel like you have to do this or something bad will happen. For instance, if you don't go to church, you're going to hell. If you don't go to college, you'll never get a good job. If you don't eat your veggies, you won't grow to be big and strong. If you're not good then Santa won't bring you any gifts. etc etc.

Those are just small level scare tactics, none of those things are facts. They're things told to you in effect to control you and create this form of submission so that you don't seek independence and don't contemplate rebellion for fear of repercussions. My depression actually led to me becoming more insightful. My depression empowered me to not let fear dictate my life. My depression encouraged me to not just live life by these standards that I allowed to haunt me. These standards made me second guess myself. These standards made me feel inadequate. These standards made me regret life. These standards made me not realize that I'm an individual. As an individual I'm free to be what I want to be. I'm free to not be like anybody else. I'm free to walk my own path. I'm free to think for myself. I'm free to be free. The comfort from being free propelled me to greater heights.

As I laid on the couch in the basement, I decided to shun all the normalities I had been force fed. I decided to live for me and only do things that felt right in my mind and heart without the fear of being judged or ridiculed. I decided to not let fear ever force me to give up hope. I decided to take chances. I decided to take risks. I decided to live life only as I wanted to live it. This was my time to say to heck with standards and what's "practical" or "acceptable" I just wanted to be happy. You never realize how important happiness is until you're sitting alone with your thoughts without being able to do the things you enjoy. It angered me to know that all this time, this production was going on around me. Why wasn't I informed of what was going on? Why are these standards placed on us and for us to live up to?

When you hit your opinion of "rock bottom" there's nowhere to go but up. This was my rock bottom. I'm not sure if I adequately depicted the picture of how traumatizing it was to lose the ability to simply WALK. The pain in my ankle kept me up countless night. It was such a helpless feeling. Everything was a chore. Making it to the bathroom was a task. Taking a shower was a task. Needless to say I wasn't up for the task. It's a lot harder than it sounds and 10 times harder than it looks. The next time you see a person in a wheelchair appreciate the fact that that's not you and admire the fact that in the time it took them to get ready that morning you could have got ready 5 times over. Walking is something we do everyday and take for granted everyday. We never take the time to realize how vital it is. Without being able to walk, I became far more helpless than I have ever been but much like many other people with permanent or temporary ailments, I became resourceful, I became stronger, I became better, I became ME.

CHAPTER
III

Realizing my Gift

Once I crashed into the my own version of Truman's wall, walked up the ladder and kicked it over, life changed. The view from atop was a little murky to start with. Wasn't much up there. It was just a huge vacant space. A blank canvas if you will. It wasn't immediately apparent what I would put in this space. Little did I know, but the plan for my life was in motion long before I took that wrong step on the courts of the Preston Center.

One thing about my dad that I've always loved, admired and respected was his ability to sing. On Sunday, him singing solos in the church choir was a must see. Whenever you saw "Eddie Clack" in that church program you knew at that moment something special was in store. One of the favorite songs that my dad used to perform was "Order my steps" by GMWA Women of Worship.

Today is June 26th, 2016 10:46am and as I'm editing this chapter it just occured to me the irony of how me taking the wrong step led to me devoting my life to a higher power and allowing that higher power to order my steps. At that time in my life when I got hurt, I wasn't on the right path, I wasn't cognizant of other people as much as I should have been. There was this shallow bubble and thin veil that I was living under. Listening to this song and reading the lyrics just now made me realize how powerful life is when your destiny presents itself and you follow it. I've always loved that song but never realized that that song was the message of my journey. Right now, I'm immersed in an insatiable feeling of gratitude and affirmation that I'm doing right with my life. Thank you Lord.

Order my steps in Your word dear Lord,
lead me, guide me everyday,
send Your anointing, Father I pray;
order my steps in Your word,
please, order my steps in Your word

I want to walk worthy,
my calling to fulfill.
Please order my steps Lord,
and I'll do Your blessed will.
The world is ever changing,
but You are still the same;
if You order my steps, I'll praise Your name.

Four scores and 12 years ago, I humbly stumbled upon one of my infinite talents; writing poetry. Writing poetry became a coping mechanism that I had adopted during my frosh year of college fresh off my introductory bout of depression. Writing was therapeutic, It became a daily habit to jot pages of poems into my journal. Whenever I had downtime or when a thought came to mind, I'd just sit and write. Poetry became a heavily invested passion of mine. One of the things I love most in life is to be creative. The ability to detail my feelings and thoughts into a pattern that rhymed was super cool to me. Over the course of time I started to post my poetry on Face and the book. The feedback and report that it built with my peers was amazing. Majority of my content I posted centered around Life and Love --Um, now feels as good of a time as any to mention how I spent the entire summer of 2011=ish typing of all my poetry journals into a book that I entitled "Life and Times of Love."-- The most fulfilling and reassuring aspect of posting and sharing my work on Face and the book was that it made me aware of how relatable we all are. We all want love. We all have been in love. We all have lost love and/or have had to deal with rough patches in life. I was vulnerable enough to open up and and shared all those times through my poetry.

Writing poetry initiated my forray into pursuing music. Songs are in itself another form of poetry accompanied by sound so the transition came natural. I've always enjoyed music. In middle school, I used to record songs off the radio onto cassette tapes, listen to them repeatedly and write out the lyrics to each song. Next to sports, music was my passion. I've always just appreciated how music can dictate, influence or console whatever mood that you're in. Regardless of how you feel, there's a song to complement that emotion. My siblings and I grew up singing in a local gospel choir, it wasn't something that I loved to do because I'm an introverted shy person but It was a good childhood experience. It introduced me to how powerful music can be. It was interesting to look out into the audience and see people crying, rejoicing and excited from just watching us perform. (Big ups to everybody who was in MGMC. Louisville we in here baby!)

Gospel music was the first genre I was introduced to but R&B and later on Rap music would speak to my core. My teen years were spent idolizing Tupac. An absurd amount of time was spent listening to his music and emulating his rap demeanor. The crazy thing is that it wasn't until after he "died" that I grew into a bigger fan. It was amazing to me that he had the foresight to look at life in a wider scope and in a sense live in preparation of his death. Much like how I mentioned in the prologue, I've adopted that same goal. Leaving a legacy is such a profound accomplishment. I don't want my death to be the end of me. Much like Tupac was and still is relevant after his "death" I want to leave the same impact with my life over time. In 2007-ish, before I got hurt, much like my idol before me, I decided that music would become my platform to reach immortality. In all honesty, it started off as a joke, not something I took serious or had even considered pursuing before in life. Around this time I had re-enrolled back into college. I ended up meeting and working with this kid named JR at this telemarketing office. JR was an aspiring rapper and had a whole set up in his dorm room to record music. Him and another kid named AR, who also worked with JR and I, began to hang out based on our common passion for music. One day at work, AR, JR and myself came up with this concept to do a song together. The most popular song at that time was "Duffle Bag Boy" performed by Playaz Square. We decided to make a work related parody of that song called "No Rebuttals." During work, we were always instructed by our supervisors to "rebuttal" when talking on the phone with clients. Our company objective was to sell customers on the idea to upgrade their cable services by adding movie channels to their package. If a customer declined initially, we'd provide additional information to convey to them how great of a deal this was; this method was referred to as a "rebuttal". None of my co-workers enjoyed doing this or enjoyed how the supervisors would walk around and always yell out "rebuttal, rebuttal, rebuttal..." That gave us the ammunition to create a song detailing our work oppression. We recorded the song, played it in the parking lot after work one day while everybody was gathered outside and gave an impromptu performance standing on top of our motor vehicles. It was an instant office hit. People obviously could relate with the song and the creativity of it. We were on to something. It should be stated that another artist I admired was Weird Sal Stojavic. I loved how he'd turn popular songs into parodies. That sparked the creativity in me to began to do the same. Even before doing "No Rebuttals" I had already contrived parody songs in my head but just hadn't recorded them. Eventually I would add to my arsenal of parody songs with such gems as "Stayin With My Moma" a parody of "Stuntin Like My Daddy" by Lil Wine & Birdguy; "Student Loans" a parody of "Shoulder Lean" by Young Pro and later on "My Diddy" which was a homage to music mogul Jean Puffy Cowns and parody of the song "My Dougie" performed by ???. Here it was. My life's plan revealing itself.

Now that I was well on my way to establishing myself as a cultural phenomenon and the next Tupac, I needed a moniker. Coming up with an alter ego and name to envision thousands of screaming female fans yelling out was harder than I imagined. The first name I came up with was "LB" which stood for Lois's (my mom) baby and/or " Louisville Born". The name sounded cool until I referred to myself as that aloud. The next option was going by the primary name that people knew me as, "Clack". Only issue there was that in the music world, the artist name of "Clack" was already taken by my brother LaVon. Knowing I couldn't go by "Clack" was a crushing blow but I stayed steadfast in my quest to create a name that would transcend and connect with the masses. Had to scrap all previous ideas and get back to the drawing board. For those of us who were college students in 2005, and for whom Face and the book was created for, you all can recall the popular practice of creating a pseudo middle name. The name I elected in those days was "God's Gift". Often times I caught flack because people thought "God's Gift" came from a cocky or arrogant place as to say I was God's gift to the world because I was tall, dark and handsome but to me it meant that life is a gift from God and that my life was "God's gift". To save myself the hassle of constantly explaining myself, I changed it "Gift". While sitting at the drawing board, I felt like "Gift" would be a cool name to go by but I wanted it to mean something deeper than just a name. I literally wanted it to mean something. I spent time jotting down ideas then it came to me like a song I wrote:

Good.
Intentions.
For.
Talented.

Cause

God.
Intended.
For.
This.

Through everything I had been through in life; dealing with suicidal thoughts and depression, I never lost my spirituality. It was apparent that my life wasn't meant to be regular. Failing to kill myself twice was evidence that I'm here for a reason. My talent was God given. It was my intention to do good things with it because this was what God intended.

This was God's plan.

As I stood in my vacant space staring at my blank canvas, I started to envision things to add. Music was the first but I knew it wouldn't be the last. I reverted back to writing. My journal turned from a notebook into contrived pieces of art I'd type into my cellular device and save. Others I'd construct in the notes section of Face and the book and post. Unlike the first collection of poems, these weren't as dark and dreary, these were written with self-evaluation, self-perspective and self-purpose. Through writing I was able to express those dark times but also illustrate the triumph in overcoming those arduous scenarios and be defiant to the odds stacked against me:

December 16,2008 ·

My failed suicide attempts... still talkin sh❊t to my wrist...

If i died how many would care that i was no longer alive??
I think it's human to fantasize about suicide
i've had my time
well it was plural
so let me say times
and if i wasn't so "arrogant"and "conceited" then I would've probably tried
lol(inside joke)
cause I ain't scared to die
but the easy way out isn't always the right objective
but i'm sensitive to pain and pressure
sometime I put it off for months at a time and neglect it
but there days 2 at a time out of the year
when I disappear
close down from the world around me, sit and shed a tear
listen to the Canton Sprituals sing
"I WONT COMPLAIN"
look to the sky and ask God to relieve my fear
sniffle, swing my fist against the wind and reflect
have a gut check with my chest
look on the inside and confront my pride
i've lost loved ones and it's been days later where I still haven't cried
I bottle up a lot..but reality creeps up twist the cap and I bust and explode like pop
but life ain't pose to be peachy keen... there's happiness and joy, but some heartache and pain in between
I thank God for my positivity optimism and hindsight
cause u only get one life
but i'm an overachiever so I might die twice
but it won't be for not
cause as I see it I got 2 purposes in life, to live and to pass
so I don't live in the past
but it's complicated cause some females aren't impressed by my laugh
"you take er'thing as a joke, I can neva know when to take you serious"

and the ones who know me are probably knoddin in agreeance if they
hearin this
or better yet seeing it
my mind is a mess and I don't feel like cleaning it.
there more things to be concerned with dear
ppl starvin
ppl dyin
ppl homeless livin under a bridge or missin and ain't been seen in years
so pardon me if i dnt get mad or make a fuss.
am I selfish cause I preference ME before us??
I was born alone so imma die alone, handle my problems on my own
cause at the end of the day all I got is me and all you got is you
so don't stress cause I ain't called or came through
I just see the bigger picture
life is a verse I wrote so let me read my scripture
not tryna diss ya or dismiss ya or to the curb kick ya
but i'm dreamin and you shake me tryna wake me
jus follow me you ain't gotta chase me
but if it fits you well then erase me
I make tissue of an issue cause it really ain't shit
if i'm still livin how can I be missed??
and it ain't gotta be a holiday for me to show my G.I.F.T
my life is poor but my mind is rich
I shouldn have to tell you I care, you should feel it when we kiss
or when I mix that black with the white
and tell you what's real and how I feel whether I text it or type
but you right
I am a lil too complex from the outside looking in
but I understand me perfectly, i'm my own best friend
my own next of kin
Kanye said it best:
"I"LL LOOK IN THE MIRROR IF I NEED SOME HELP"
but I took it a further step and wrote my will to myself
I recycle watches cause I hate wasting time
love is blind
so i'd rather be truthful than to pull the wool over ya eyes and tell lies
I ain't like most guys

I'll tell you straight up if my only intention is between ya thighs
call it what chu will..but I won't tamper with how u feel
play ya cards and then we can deal
its cliche to say but i keep it real
I ain't too tough to admit that somedays I feel like shit
hold a knife in my hand and talk shit to my wrist
like" I outta f*ck you up b*tch"
its therapy cause I know i'd neva take it that far
that's just a metaphor don't take it literal ya'll, no scar no marks
no tape no chalk
I think fast so it mumbles my words when I talk
you might think my marbles are lost, but they in reach
I just lose inhibitions when I speak
the true truth sets you free, I rather it be said than left unheard.
I pour liquor from myself er'time I see a curb
I make definitions out of my own word
cause who knows, I might mess around and die next week
before I reach my peak
but i'm prepared mentally in my memory
only heaven knows when imma go
but don't remember me
jus re-memory
thank of me when you think of me.

CHAPTER
IV

Landing

Location: Los Angeles, CA
Date: April 5, 2010
Day 1

The wheels finally tapped the runway at LAX culminating my 4 hour nonstop flight across the country. My eyes opened. I peered out the window to the left of me and stared out into the night. Out of my element. Out of my comfort zone. Is a perfect description of how I felt as I gazed through that window. To say I was nervous would be the epitome of an understatement. This unknown reality that awaited me created unprecedented levels of anxiety. I was beyond worried. Beyond feeling leery of what laid ahead. There I sat. My mind racing a million seconds a minute. Alone in my cocoon of fear. Complete silence. Then a ding. The ding of the seatbelt sign going off is similar to the sound of a cap gun at a track and field event; everybody sprints to grab their luggage from the overhead compartment, hurdle over seats and race down the aisle to the exit. It didn't have that effect on me. I just sat there. Motionless. There was no rush. There was no sense of urgency. There was nowhere I had to go. Nothing I had to do. No clue of what I would do once I exited the plane. No clue where I would go on a daily basis. No clue what I would do on a nightly basis. The biggest adjustment I knew I had to conquer was how to survive. There wasn't a safety net. No fall back plan. No exit strategy. Nothing. My intentions were to land and let things manifest. This journey was predicated on having blind faith in what I believed in and not what others believed in.

This was me trusting my instincts. This was me being prepared for the worst and not fathoming the best. I didn't want this to be easy. I wanted this to be the worst thing ever and I'm proud to say that it was just that.

"Your biggest trials turn into your biggest triumphs"

One undertaking from this journey and what I hope to share as well as convey through my story, is to never take for granted another person's struggle. Unless you're in their shoes, you'll never know. You'll never know until you step out of your comfort zone and live it. Your perspective and outlook on life won't help but to change once you experience it. Those 26 days were unequivocally the best WORST thing to ever happen to me. It changed my perspective and outlook on a myriad of life issues.

It'd be advantageous to say I hit the ground running. I didn't. Those who know me will tell you being timid isn't part of my acumen. However, this was the most timid I'd ever been in life. So much doubt. So much hesitance. So much cause and concern. So many variables to factor in.

My mom always tells me:

"The best way to find your way around is to get lost"

All of this is documented because as I mentioned, or maybe I haven't mentioned yet, but I kept a video diary, I would routinely just recap my days or just cut the camera on and talk about how horrible of time I was having and how much the ish sucked. I'll share the transcripts of those entries as we go along.

This trip was the quintessential paradigm of me doing just that. The two things I remember most vividly when I finally built up the cojones to step foot outside of the airport was how amazing it was to finally see a palm tree and most importantly how cold it was!!!!! Color me a naive country boy from Kentucky because I sure as heck figured that LA had 80 degree weather year round; completely missed that memo. By golly, it was April for pete's sake. Sheeseh. Here comes lil ole me negating the simple tidbits of traveling like uh, checking the weather! My wardrobe of basketball shorts and a cotton hoodie didn't stand a chance in this weather. It's my typical traveling ensemble aside from the fact I usually wear some form of jogging pants but since I was flying to LA, I figured I'd spruce things up by opting to depart from jogging pants in favor of basketball shorts. Bad idea. Kentucky's humidity makes 50 degrees bearable. In California, 50 degrees is categorized as a winter storm. That being said, only complainers complain so I thought warm thoughts and forged my way through the storm.

For the next 40 minutes I walked around lost. Well, lost is a relative term, I wasn't lost, I was more so walking around without any attempts to find out where I was going. My wandering stroll was utilized to become one with the elements and soak into my surroundings. It was slowly starting to hit me that I reached the place of no return. The next three weeks and five days would be spent doing this very same thing. These are the journeys that turn men into boys and at that time I was a full fledge man and had the stomach hairs to prove it. I pride myself on being a competitive person so I was locked in and mentally prepared for whatever the night brings.

Plenty wandering and wrong turns later I was able to matriculate my way to the bus stop on 96th and Sepulveda. That bus stop set the stage for my introduction to the homeless culture. There was a conclave of homeless people resting on the benches and other areas around the bus compound. This was their life, the life I was there to adopt. There was one gentleman in particular who I fixated my eyes on. Pause. "Pops" is what I nicknamed him. He drew a striking resemblance to the character John Witherfork played in the movie franchise "Thursday." Unlike John Witherfork's character, he sported a scruffy grey beard to accompany the group of spiders having a meeting on his head. He was dressed in the rudimentary homeless garb; 3-4 pairs of pants accompanied by a blazer and light jacket worn over a hoodie. To finish off his ensemble, he sported a pair of white running shoes without laces . Pops sat there engaging in a one sided dialogue with another gentleman. I couldn't understand his rhetoric, in fact, I'm not sure If he was using real words or speaking in complete coherent sentences. The gentleman he was speaking with was attentive to whatever he was saying and nodded to the cadence of his speech. Pops was sitting on a cement bench leaning back with his legs crossed. His persona was that of such which exudes confidence and comfort. Once you get accustomed to something, that becomes your environment, your calm and your peace. To him, he wasn't loitering or just sitting on a bus stop, he was at home. He was comfortable and felt no apprehension about his situation. It's hard not to appreciate and admire the simple act of others doing what they have to do to survive. Sitting outside all day with nowhere to go isn't an easy reality to adjust to and I knew my time to adjust was now.

Due to the obvious fact that I'm not from LA, I wasn't really sure which bus to catch nor smart enough to ask anybody which bus to catch to get to downtown LA where the gym I signed up for was.(Yes. I got a gym membership, I didn't go there to be that kind of homeless) Luckily, I had an app on my cellular device (Yes. I had my phone with me, I didn't go there to be that kind of homeless.) that gave me a list of buses from 96th and Sepulveda that would take me downtown, one of which being the 40. After like 35 minutes, the 40 finally pulls into the bus compound, pulls up to the curb and stops. After 4 minutes and 19 seconds of me standing waiting for the doors to open, the bus pulls off without letting anybody on. I stood there confused and dumbfounded while watching the bus drive away. It was my assessment that maybe that wasn't the right bus. That was my overall consensus until I watched the bus pull around to the other side. It stopped, opened it's doors and let passengers on. It became apparent to me that I evidently was standing on the wrong side! In a haste, I dashed across the bus compound to cut the bus off. If anybody here knows football, it's like angling a tackle. The objective is to run to the spot where you'll meet the runner and be able to either tackle them or trip them up. I did this to perfection. As I rounded my way around the center structure of the bus compound there was the bus. There was me in hot pursuit preparing to square my shoulders and launch myself into the bus like former NFL Ravens linebacker Jay Lewis. I see the bus driver. The bus driver sees me. In my mind I'm thinking: "ok, cool, he's going to stop. No worries." He had already started to slowly drive away but it was my expectation that he'd see me and stop. Confident that that would occur, I stopped running and stood with my arm extended to give him a nonverbal gesture of "Hey bro, I'm not from here, this is my first time ever being in this city, I'm homeless and just trying to make my way downtown." Apparently he didn't speak this form of nonverbal gestures and instead countered with a nonverbal gesture of his own that I could only interpret as "If you see kay you" followed by a Heisman trophy worthy stiff arm as he proceeded to high step up the sideline. The crazy aspect of all this is that I was literally close enough to touch the door of the bus. All he had to do was stop and let me on. Not only didn't he stop but he tapped the gas while passing me. I turned to Toto and said:

"We're not in Kentucky anymore."

After my abysmal attempt of hailing a bus, another bus pulls up. It's not the bus I need but I approached the driver and asked if he knew when the next 40 was coming. He informed me that they run every hour. Now that I had a determined allotted amount of time to wait, I decided to do something to eradicate my feeling of hunger by venturing out into the brisk night in search of nourishment. My brief trek took me down Century Blvd but I didn't detect any places in sight and decided to head back to the bus stop. As I was walking, I saw a bright sign off in the deep distance. At first sight, I was perceiving it to be a sign from God but it was in actuality a Burger Queen sign. According to my calculations, I could go there, eat, sit down, relax and momentarily escape the frigid night all in time to catch the next bus. During the course of walking towards BQ, I noticed shadowy figures lined up along the sidewalk up ahead. The closer I got I observed that there was a line of five or six homeless people lying on the sidewalk in succession. As I walked past them I developed this nostalgic sobering feeling. It's not like I've never seen homeless people before but not to this magnitude. This sight, albeit shocking to me at the time, pales in comparison to when I went to skid row for the first time.

While spending that one week and 19 days homeless days in LA, I journeyed to skid row one night and was just mesmerized by everything. That time spent walking past all those people and seeing rats running up the sidewalk was insane to me. One bright moment, if you can call it that, was that on the corner of the street I walked down, there was a church that was having an evening service. You could hear gospel music playing from the outside. I took a moment and just stood there with my eyes closed listening to the harmonious sounds of some of the people outside clapping and singing along. It was incredibly uplifting that even in their circumstance they had that spirit.

To this day, November 12th, 2015 8:39am I have NEVER seen anything as disheartening as what I witnessed that night! To put it in words is going to be laborious. You really have to witness it in person to get the full scope of how astonishingly depressing it is. It honestly makes me emotional and angry just to even think about. Excuse my french but how in the FUDGE is this even possible in a city where houses get sold for tens of millions of dollars, and blockbuster movies get made? How in the FUDGE are people allowed to live like this? Sure some of these people, for lack of better words, kind of bring it on themselves but if we can send millions in dollars and relief to other countries, why the FUDGE can't we do that in Los Angeles? That's what I strongly dislike about society. Whenever a tragedy happens -- I'm not going to name any specifics because I don't want to come off like I'm rationalizing one tragedy being more relevant or substantial than the other-- but something will happen and they'll hold telethons, food drives, clothing drop offs and take monetary donations for these once occurring things as they should but for something that is occurring everyday there isn't a public outcry to fix it or do something consistently to rectify the situation? Why isn't a facility being built to house these people? WHY SWAY? One of my life goals is to build a huge a** warehouse with showers, restrooms, cots, heating, AC as well as other amenities and let homeless people stay there. It'd be structured and things would be expected of them but it'll just be a place to get people off the streets. When I was walking the streets hours on end sleep deprived, the one thing I desired more than anything was just a place to go to sleep. I wanted so bad just to lay down. You guys will never know that feeling of being sleepy but not able to go to sleep. It's one of the worst feelings ever. I would of done anything just to have a place where I knew I could close my eyes without fear of being attacked or kicked out. I wanted comfort. In other cities like New York and Chicago, it gets insanely cold during the winter, where do those homeless people you see on the streets in the summer go when it's cold? Where do they go when it it's raining? Where can they go for safety and shelter? In my astute opinion, places like skid row shouldn't even exist. Granted, It's impossible to help everybody. There are millions of people with issues who also need help and attention.

Growing up in a family of 7, I was privy to plenty help and attention. Both of my parents were on disability; my father from having hurt his back working for a roofing company and my mother due to heart and back complications that prevented her from working. As a kid, having my mom give my siblings and I each a 1 dollar food stamp for us to go to the store and purchase candy or little deborah cakes for 25 cents so that my mother could take that change, allow it to accumulate then use it to buy the things you couldn't buy with food stamps such as soap, toilet paper or cleaning supplies influenced my outlook on helping others. I remember getting that toy from the Salvation Army at 8 years old. I remember being a part of that "Angel tree" where they'd write the names of families who needed help on a white angel shaped card and hang them on this big tree. My family's name was on that tree. We would get clothes,canned goods and other items from people who donated these things to the families on the tree. Without others helping me and my family, where would I be? Those things never leave my mind. I'm reminded each time I see the Salvation Army representatives set up outside of the grocery. I make it my priority to always give them money because I want that 8 year old to receive the same toy I received. Paying it forward was ingrained in me long before I was even aware of it.

This journey was a sacrifice; not something I had or needed to do but something I WANTED to do. Something that I knew would have a fervent and everlasting effect on me. In the few years prior to this journey, I wasn't the person I am now today. In the few years after this journey I wasn't the person I am now today. There have been a lot of dark times for me but in those dark times I was able to see the light at the end of the tunnel. I was able to have intuition and maintain my level of having humanity and compassion for others. That's what my journey exemplifies. This is for a higher purpose. My hands are typing these words. My mind aren't thinking these thoughts. It's bigger than me. I'm vessel of good deeds. A vessel of positivity. A vessel of optimism, motivation and inspiration. it's something I wholeheartedly accept and have devoted my life to. It's my hope that positivity starts to win out over all the negative things that continuously occur in life and what people clamour to.

Don't ignore love.

Don't ignore life.

Don't ignore liberty.

Don't ignore those who are continuously ignored.

CHAPTER
V

Pick me up

Location: Los Angeles, CA
Date: April 6th, 2010
Day 1-2

After enjoying fine dining feasting on a double cheeseburger and an icee, courtesy of BQ, I made my way to the bus stop and THIS time the bus let me on. whooooohoooo!!! That bus ride was informative. I gazed out the window observing things I had only heard about in rap songs like Thinburger and 7-12. The persons on the bus were good subjects to grab intel from. It was my intent to blend in and not stick out. I was leary of people smelling bama on me and trying to run up on me for set tripping. Again, I had no idea where I was going, I just wanted to get downtown. When the bus finally let me off downtown I was surprised to see how vacant and desolate downtown Los Angeles looked. Didn't expect to see how run down those buildings looked. The storefronts were covered with those metal doors they pull down. Wherever you go, in any city, when you see those you know you're in a bad part of town. The streets were laced with homeless people wandering around and sleeping on the sidewalks at seemingly every turn. As I walked, I absorbed the atmosphere attempting to digest what I was witnessing.

By making great use of modern technology I utilized this map app on my cellular device and was able to reach my gym and what I expected to be my safe haven for the night. The NAME of this gym in question was highly misleading. The primary reason for joining this gym in question was because the NAME of the gym in question gave me the impression that it was a place I could go at any HOUR of the day and that this gym in question would be open. It wasn't until I arrived at one of this gym in question's 5th and Flowers location, that I learned that there was clear fineprint that I omitted once agreeing to terms and conditions. It was well within reason for me to assume that this gym in question would be OPEN once I arrive. There's 24 hours in a day and the gym in question gave me false hopes that even at this hour of 1am that this gym in question would be OPEN. Nope! In fact, by that time the gym in question had been closed for 4 hours. No worries. The gym in questioned opened at 5am so I only had like 4 hours to kill before I could go there. At this point in time, I was a novice in the art of time killing. Present day, I'm like the grand wizard of time killing. That 5 days and three week experience conditioned me for it. It taught me how to be resourceful using the tricks of the trade to become the master of all I survey. Those 240 minutes went by surprisingly fast. I just sat outside rapping songs in my head and walked around for a little bit. Finally, it was time, I ventured into the gym in question, used the bathroom and sat around for a second. The ambiance of the gym in question wasn't what I expected,. The lockers weren't big enough to fit my backpack in and something just wasn't right so I left. There was a food court outside of the gym in question which came in handy because I utilized the power outlets to charge my cellular device, which by this time was dead, as I indulged on some Mcdowell's breakfast. All in all my first night wasn't too bad. Unfortunately, I can't say the say for the next night:

Location: Los Angeles, CA
Date: April 7th, 2010 2:19 am
Day 3

soumyea uh
Cam's been dead for like....shisshs...

(pauses)

...probably like the last 10 hours but I finally found a place to uh, plug it in, well a plug that works but uhh, it's been uh, (sucks teeth) it's been a rough night man...

(long pause)

...I don't even know how to explain it really, it's just...

just odd (grunts)

it's like (laugh)

I'm here, but I'm..

(pauses)

...nowhere to go, ah um..

(Sucks teeth)

...like I don't think i've ever been this vulnerable in my life, it's not.-- I'm subject to anything, but uh there's really nothing. I don't have control over nothing really. but uh, yea, I think last time I was trying to check in like when it went dead, I was like um, I forgot.. I mean there's nothing to do. I got to kill time. I ain't built the gusto to sleep on the streets yet plus it's cold see I just um, hopped on a bus to go downtown so I went downtown, uhh, I got some

good sleep on that bus tho. Then I just rode that same bus back to where I was at. It took off about a good uhh 2 hours off there's like no, uh, time is so irrelevant. There's, there's so many hours in the day but what do you need hours for if you got nothing to do with them? Like I don't have nothing to do, nowhere to go, so it just makes the hours so so like dreadful, it's just like, just imagine like it's never ending, it's just, aw I can't even describe it, it's like, there's no end it's, like you know like if you go to work, you go to school, your day ends bow, you're done. But you're just outside all day, walking around doing nothing, like you, when do you stop? And I'm not sleeping, last night I didn't sleep at all. I figure the time I slept at the gym with my hand on my head for 20 minutes, bus, probably like 40 mins, like a hour in 2 and a half days almost. So it's just weird, but yeah man I just feel, I don't know, I feel just (pauses) alone like look, it's just me...

(voice cracks)

...nobody's here, and I was saying earlier you take so much for granted...

(pauses)

...I take a lot for granted and I admit I take a lot for granted... the whole.. well not the whole, well I say the whole (point) just to like test myself see what I'm made of see what uh I can attest to be accountable for my strength, my resiliency. It's pretty, I don't know, I aint broke down yet, I'm borderline. You can probably tell my voice is shaky now cause I don't want to cry. I mean I cried, nah I haven't cried since I been here, I cried when I, I cried, I cried before my flight tho, I aint gon lie man I was scared to death, I'm hmm, nah I, I wasn't, I was internally scared , I was worried, anxious I didn't know how to feel but umm yeah (laugh) I, I'm sitting outside a building, with, charging,

I'm out outside a building. I'm not at home, i'm not with somebody I know, i'm just out here man ....

(long pause)

...oop and there goes a tear....

(long pause)

(deep sigh)

...thugs cry too... that ain't a cry that's.. I don't.. cause like.. I don't get frustrated, I don't get umm none of those negative things, I don't get agitated, I just get like, uh, alright more, that's just more more to add on, but like, when you start, when you start in a negative then you add negatives onto it it just, it overwhelms you. Like it's bad enough i'm here by myself like, like, by myself so it ain't like, I got no kind of support.. well I got support but it ain't like somebody here next to me like keeping me focused. oh yeah, I met this um this other homeless lady I don't know she might have been crazy then she might have of been, significant. but anyway she um, she walks past me, she's like, I mean, she was speaking to everybody so she walked past me and she's like:

"you looking good tonight"

I'm like "thank you"..."appreciate it"

and then um I don't know if she asked about a light or something whatever it is, I done forgot, I done forgot the whole story whatever she's' like, she's like

"you have big things in coming in your future"

aw that's what happened I got on a red and white shirt and she got on red and white shirt and she's like:

"I'm wearing, I'm wearing red and white too"

and i'm like "aw ok coo" then I have on a black and white um jacket and so she's like:

"I'm wearing black and white, too"

and she's like pulling on her pants, like she had a cigarette in her hand, the ashes fell off and I guess it's called uh a heart drop a heart beat, or, some kind of something, she like:

"oh when if something happens like that that means something special will happen"

then she's like:

"many blessings to come" and just walked off.

I was like "wow" maybe if that was like a sign like, know what i'm saying? cause all day I, I don't want to say doubting myself but all day been like:

"What am I doing? what am I doing?"

like seriously, like:

"Who does this?"...

(laughs)

and then she came along and she had came back actually like, like 30 minutes later she was saying she's an angel and that um and I had big things on the horizon,

72

many blessings to come and I took it for what it's worth but you never know man some say the lord works in mysterious ways, and this something I've, I've always wanted to, to do this, to come to come and be, I don't just, just guess homeless but to come on a whim and just see what happens. This only day 2 of like twenty.. so I ain't really like, I ain't started started I really ain't done nothing. You can't settle in on being homeless but I don't got no routine I don't know where I''m going half the time, I'm pretty sure probably ya know, matriculate some more things as time wears on and then who knows, but yeah...

(pause)

(singing)

> *..."this is the softer side of me"...*

> *I'm still a thug tho shawty, but yeah I don't be filming as much real I'm just trying to soak it all in, let it build up, but yeah...*

> *...this all a work in progress...*

> *...this is just my process.*

The level of vulnerability I felt at that moment was unreal. The world just appeared much larger than I had ever envisioned it. It was such a stark contrast to realize that in that moment, in a sense, my life didn't matter. My life as it was didn't exist anymore. There was no getting home from work. There was no going to the gym or hanging with friends. There was no watching tv. There was no normalcy. I didn't exist. I was just there. Alone. I had never felt so alone. It startled me. It terrified me. Staring out into the night I didn't see one thing that looked familiar. I didn't see anything that made me feel at ease. I couldn't relate to the atmosphere I was in. I literally didn't know where I was. We've all been lost before. The de facto logical next step when lost is to ask for directions. This luxury wasn't afforded to me. I had got turned around trying to find the gym but there was a destination. As I sat there in the corner of that building I had no destination. I didn't have anything to comfort or console me; expect for my tears.

CHAPTER
VI

Misconceptions and Perceptions

December 1, 2015

It's currently 1:31pm on a cold and rainy Tuesday here in Brooklyn, NY on Flatbush Ave. Stationed in Stardollars, across from Senior's where those one kids from that one show had to walk to get cheescake. These coffee chain restaurants have been the unofficial hub and workspace for me while I've been writing this book. I want an endorsement deal once this book comes out. Make sure my flight to Seattle is an aisle seat. I'm tall.

Those minute details aside, I spent the entire morning commuting from Irvington, NJ where my little sister Lydia, who I flew here from LA last Friday to visit lives. Before leaving California, I reached a satisfactory stopping place and decided to send the first few chapters to my family and a few other people to share and get feedback from. My plan for while I was away from the city of angels was to not do any additional writing. Instead I decided that I'll take this time to review and edit what I had written thus far. Much like everything else in life, it's all subject to change. There was a new ambiance and feeling that struck me when I got to New York that offered me insight. It sparked my mind to share additional life content that I felt I really needed to mention.

On Saturday, my sister and I watched "The Truman Show" She had mentioned that she hadn't watched it before after she read the first few chapters of my manuscripts when I make reference to the movie. I found it on demand so we watched it. It had been 6 or 7 years since I had seen the movie. After watching the movie, I noticed an inaccuracy in something I alluded to. Truman walked up a flight of stairs and not up a ladder as I had previously stated. While watching the movie I found additional commonalities between my life and the movie. It's kind of eerie. It reminded me of feelings I expressed when going through the genesis of my depression. In one scene, after Truman hits the wall with the boat and fights against the wall trying to break though, he then gets out of the boat, walks along the wall and comes to a staircase. As he is about to exit, the voice of the producer of the show "Christoff" speaks to him, within that dialogue Truman turns to the camera, after having his back turned listening to Christoff, and asks:

"... Who am I?""

"...Is nothing real...?"

Those were the same things I once pondered. I wanted answers. I wanted to know. That same inquisitive demeanor is still present in me. There are a lot of things I don't understand and can't fathom. Earlier today, a person I had befriended here in NY named Nat expressed to me how she lost the desire to see me. It caught me off guard, I didn't feel as if I had done anything to warrant that sentiment. What I learned is that for some people, if you're not available in the manner in which they want you to be available then you're disposable. It's crazy the amount of arrogance and lack of humility that some people have. They treat people as if they're some sort of commodity and only associate with them if there's some sort of direct benefit. Whatever happened to being genuine? Whatever happened to doing good deeds? Whatever happened to respecting others? Life isn't guaranteed, tomorrow isn't either but there are individuals with smug demeanors who are quick to sort of distance themselves from others in a manner of making it seem as if those people aren't good enough for them.

For me, I'm not that type of person. I keep in touch with the people I share an initial genuine bond with even if it's every few months. In the grand scheme of things, life is relative, subjective and perspective based. My perspective is never that of a constant need for attention. How I feel about a person doesn't change with the lack of time spent together. It's not my belief that you have to foster relationships and express sentiments continually. My best friends are people I rarely talk to or even see. We have that bond where we understand each other and it's like no time has been lost in the gaps of us not speaking or seeing each other. We can not talk for months and there will be no angst. There aren't "Why haven't you called or texted me?" instances. It's almost like people need your constant attention to gauge your interest. That's never been my thing. My memory isn't the best but I don't forget people or try to forget people. There's room for everybody. I believe in giving people the right and free range to be themselves and to be in their life regardless of if it's to my benefit or not. Encouragement is the most exciting thing for me to offer. My advice is to ignore everything and everyone in favor of doing what makes you happy, even if it's to my own detriment. Personal satisfaction reigns supreme to me. I've experienced it, I'd be remiss not to encourage others to take that leap of faith and to encourage them to take that journey to get to know themselves on a supreme level.

What I've learned about myself as of late is that I bond best with strangers. There's so much information to obtain and exchange. People who don't know you can give you unbiased truths, help you gain perspective as well as insight and also allow you to measure yourself in contrast to the things that come up in conversation. With getting to know people, more personal questions are asked. More interest goes into what you're telling and being told. It's a genuine exchange. With people who you already know, I'm always weary of a bias of if this person is saying this with a motive or if that's truly their assertion of what I'm informing them of. Yesterday, I had lunch with Dia, who I briefly while sitting in the hotel lobby when I was in Miami this past August. Last week, before I knew I was coming to NY, I messaged her on Face and the book and sent her my number for her to contact me. She texted me later that day and we maintained a healthy dialogue over those next few days talking about life and things of that nature. When I found out I was going to come here, I informed her and she suggested that we link up. We arranged to meet up for lunch down the street from her job. We sat inside this Asian restaurant for 45 minutes basking in each other's presence. She asked some very introspective questions that made me really think and self evaluate myself. I'd consider myself to be very observing, inquisitive, and insightful. She possesses those same qualities as well as being a "smart ass" as she declared me to be during our conversations. Within these conversations she asked me:

"Are you happy?"

After explaining to her my current lifestyle, the actual content and thesis to this very book, she was intrigued and interested about how I'm able to be by myself. How I'm able to not be emotionally attached and if it was because of a family strain or lack thereof having family. She asked about my relationship goals and was actually surprised to learn that I'm a hopeless romantic. What I detailed to her was that I'm a product of my environment, albeit an environment I created. It isn't something I'm choosing to do as much as it is something I'm doing because I'm not fully able to do the things I'd really enjoy doing. In terms of relationships, I'd love to be in love, in a relationship and married with kids but that's not the reality. I've tried and I'm open to it but it's just not meant to be the case right now. This journey was never intended to last this long. People routinely ask me when I plan to stop or when I plan to settle down. I honestly don't have that answer. It's all predicated on things changing in my life. It's believed by those who know my story that I don't or can't do anything other than what I am doing. The truth is that it's out of my hands and not up to me. It's up to the universe and the environment that my current environment evolves into.

In the movie "The Truman Show" Truman's initial love interest, Slyvia was taken away from him because they wanted a different storyline to occur and she didn't fit into their plans. In one particular scene it shows him recalling the events of how they met, the times they shared together and how he had kept her sweater. The scene goes on to show when she is removed from the show and the warning she gave him:

"....It's all fake Truman.."

"... it's all for you..."

"... everybody is pretending.."

MISCONCEPTIONS AND PERCEPTIONS

Some days it feels like everybody in my life is pretending. It's rare that I feel genuine connections. When I do, I instantly cling to that. With Nat, there was an instant connection. What I believed to be genuine turned out to be superficial. Those instances often occur, so when Dia asked; "How can you travel by yourself and be so emotionally unattached?" then it's for those reasons. The reality is that I'm never alone. I'd prefer to be alone. I can function quite lovely being isolated and only being around myself. I also love being around likeminded people and having conversations where I can accept and impart wisdom to others. In my current life role, I'm in a very comfortable position because I'm on the outside looking in. I don't live in this "world." Standards and expectations mean nothing to me. It's never my desire to do what others are doing. It's never my desire to do what others think or expect me to do. Being 31, with no material possessions (ie a house, car or consistent job) is a flaw to a lot of people and something not everybody understands or even agrees with. What I'll be able to convey later on through sharing my life experiences, is that this is what works best for me. The greatest commodities to me are "Time" and "Freedom." With time and freedom I'm allowed to do what I want, when I want, how I want. People often find it weird or even suggest that I'm being dishonest when I allude to the fact that I don't get mad, or stressed out. That reason being is because I'm not influenced by the things that anger and stress people out. Most frustrations are money induced, relationship based or in regards to a job. I'm single, self employed and at one point in time I spent 624 hours living off pocket change and the bare minimum. From the outside looking in, I noticed the flaws in the world and decided to keep my distance and not to partake in it. Everybody isn't so fortunate. They allow anger and stress, which is perpetuated by fear, to consume them. What I've learned is that a person's issue with you has little to do with you. That strife and friction is their insecurities speaking for them. It's them projecting their fears on you. No fears or insecurities hamper my logic or thought process. I'm able to see and think more clearly. Having a clear mind is imperative to me because with a clear mind you can make clear and rational decisions.

Truman had the option to not walk through that door. Going through that door was going into the unknown. There was no way of knowing what was on the other side. He took a chance. He took a leap of faith.

My trip to LA was me walking through that door. It was a chance for me to shed my fears, shed my insecurities. To shed the anger, doubt, regret and remorse I had up built up. It afforded me time and freedom to find and define myself. During lunch Dia she told me she feels as if people don't start knowing who they are until they are 24. Ironically, the transitions after my injury into this newfound perspective occured when I was 24. What I learned about myself from that transition was that I need freedom.

Our vices define us. Freedom is my addiction. Fortunately for me I had the time to chase that freedom. This book is my quest to not only share my life but to also inspire others to live the life they want for themselves. We all have dreams. The key is to turn those dreams into goals. Pursue those goals. Then reach those goals. That's life. That's living life. That's living your dream. It takes accepting the qualms of taking chances. Going through bad times builds character. If you've never been through anything then in my opinion you'll never really get to know yourself or even know the people around you. During lunch I was able to talk to Dia without any filter or hesitation, prejudice or ridicule. There was genuine admiration displayed on her end as well as mine. We were able to listen to each other share our stories and offer commentary and ask questions to delve deeper into the underlying reasons of why we are the ways we are. Two relative strangers with so much in common. An equally detached demeanour and rebel nature that allows us to be content in situations that others would find uncomfortable or feel out of place in. Two relative strangers who share the same passion for writing, being expressive and find the same flaws in the world to be pretentious and annoying.

Christoff, being the creator and producer of The Truman Show, controlled everything in Truman's life. To me, Christoff represents a God complex. He literally oversaw everything that Truman did because his office was positioned high above the fictional town of "Seaview" where Truman lived. Depending on how you view things, Christoff can represent a higher power or he can represent society and the people who concoct these standards and expectations that are subtly used to control people. There's only so far you can go and so much you can do in this world without being influenced or swayed to conform of compromise your initial plan or idea. There are laws and rules to keep certain things from happening. Some of them are valid and used with the intent to protect the greater good of mankind. However, in my opinion, some of these things are also used to prevent people from realizing their own potential. Christoff did everything he could to keep the truth from Truman even if Truman died in the process as evident how he instructed for the storm to be more and more intense to scare Truman into not continuing on the boat. He created a hysteria and profound fear within Truman by faking his dad drowning to death. That kept Truman from ever thinking of leaving because the town was surrounded by water. Truman never thought about leaving because he knew he couldn't. His fear of water was too great. Once he got over that fear he took charge of his life and did exactly what he wanted to do. People either do what they want, what they're allowed to do or what they can get away with. Without the cloud of fear, a person's potential grows exponentially. But how many of us get over our fears in life? How many of us stop being held back and stop allowing others to dictate our lives for us? The system in place doesn't put people in positions to reach their full potential. We're all stiffened. Some more than others. The world we live in forces us to live up to a standard. We never question these standards, we just go along with them because as long as we've lived we were told that this is what's expected of us. I found myself questioning these standards. One thing I always wonder is Why do most people work a 9-5?

The owner of those companies people work for are millionaires, if not billionaires. These companies are worth millions, if not billions. These employees who keep these businesses afloat are told when to eat, how to dress, when they're allowed to go home but make the smallest fraction of the total company earnings. To me, that seems flawed but I get it. There's structure and structure is good. On the outside looking in, I noticed that people work hard to be able to afford the things that they feel are required (ie car, house). This hard work yields financial gain. The more money you have the more you're expected to have. You have to show your wealth. Apparently. The more you have, the more you're expected to maintain that lifestyle. Hard work turns into working even harder. Eventually, you're working 60-80 hours a week just to maintain what you have and thus sacrificing having the time to even enjoy these things you've worked so hard for. You're expected to have the bigger house and more expensive cars. These people grow to desire these things and at some point it becomes justifiable to spend ridiculous amounts of money on tedious things. We have people who buy things just because they can afford them to prove status. Then we have people who buy things they can't afford just to present status.

Based on the fact that I'm single with no kids, I'm afforded the luxury of having time to take a step back and look at the world through another lense. We live in such a selfish society. Charity is seemingly done more so for camera time or PR than it is for genuine cause and concern. So many people are worried about getting ahead and obtaining this "American Dream" that they don't assist others in their dreams and goals. It isn't until a person feels they can attain something from another person that they put forth effort and show interest in who you are as a person. My lifestyle of being a nomad gives me an honest assessment of those around me. There are quite a few people who get it but the majority of people don't. They are still consumed by standards. I don't cater to popular standard. I created my own standards. I'm aware that this is a choice and not a circumstance so I'm able to take and accept the lumps, bumps, and critique that comes with it when I tell people that I've been homeless for 5 years.

CHAPTER
VII

Balance

Location: Los Angeles. CA
Date: December 19, 2015

I've been back in La La land for a week or so and since I've been back I've been working. Gosh! Those 8 hour shifts really consume a person's day. Due to the fact that I'm a servant to public transportation, 35 minute drives to work for others are a 1 hour and 40 minute bus rides for me. Accordingly to Siri, that's roughly 12 hours everyday spent working per day. Those 12 hour days have been hijacking my time and freedom. I've felt stiffened trying to adjust to going from one extreme to another. One misconception about my situation is that it's perceived that I have no structure to my life since I don't work an everyday job or live in one central location but actually not having structure IS the structure to my life. Those who know me, know me primarily for one thing. That one thing is that there's never any telling where I might be or what I might be doing. Traveling is my structure. It's consistent. Traveling is also my passion. It's what I love to do and I'm sacrificing for it. Yesterday, I held a conversation with a person who conveyed to me that they had reservations towards me once finding out that I'm a "nomad", I've never actually referred to myself as a nomad but it's a relative word to let people know that I don't live in any one particular place and that I travel frequent, early and often. I usually just tell people I'm homeless but what I've learned is that saying you're homeless automatically means you're desolate or in despair. It's flabbergasting to most people when I share that I don't work often but yet I travel often or that I don't have a permanent residence. Telling people that you're homeless isn't as sexy as I would have imagined.

The word homeless is heavily depicted as being people who sleep in a cardboard box and panhandle. That's not the version of homeless that I am. I'm homeless because I don't own, lease or rent any property. My concept of homeless is that unless you own property, then you're homeless. Renting an apartment or paying a 30 yr mortgage to me isn't stability because there's somebody above you who dictates what you can do with that space and how long you can stay there. How can you can a place your "home" if it's a place you haven't always lived and won't always live? Nothing in life is permanent. Not even life. Those standards make people content if they have a house, car and a job but other than that what emphasis is being put on what you should have? Any emphasis on being happy? Any emphasis on building and leaving a legacy? You have a job that you break your back for, wake up early to get to and stay late to finish up for but at any moment that job can lay you off. How is that fair? I guess it beats being homeless tho, right? Me living out a backpack is my ode to freedom. My ode to not being controlled and my ode to not settling. Most people find it sketchy, some people think it's fascinating and applaud my lifestyle. This person I know in Atlanta asked me how I'm able to travel because it never seems like I'm never at work. There's this conventional wisdom that you have to do A,B,& C in life to get things done. However, I operate with a different set of letters; G,I,F & T

The physical version of me died plenty years ago. My life is like that scene in the movie "Ghost" when Patrick Swayze enters into Whoopi. There's a spirit living vicariously through me and that's what my life is. It's not me living and doing the things I want. It's me living as the higher being I believe in is directing me to live. It's crazy how when I venture to a city, it always seems like the right time for me to be there. The notion of meeting the people you're meant to meet is true to me. No matter where I am or what I'm doing, I'm going to find a way or make a way. Being in optimal control is highly important to me. That's my stability. Nobody dictates my life. Nobody tells me where I can go, what I can do. I love that. Nobody is the boss of me. If I want to travel, I don't have to worry about sick days or PTO. I don't have to get people to cover my shift. I don't have to make excuses. I don't have to lie. I can live free and true. Imagine that serenity. The bulk of you hate your jobs. The bulk of you resent your life as it is now and I'm sorry to tell you but it's because you settled. It's because the fear of living up to standards rushed you into making hasty decisions just to appease the peanut gallery. The opinions of others don't have any bearing on my happiness. My life goal and life purpose repels any negativity guided my way. It's because I'm balanced. I can't be swayed, persuaded or guilt tripped. We have to prioritize and decide which things are the best things to do and when to do it. Finding a balance is paramount.

How do you find balance?

How do we maintain balance?

How do we lose balance?

How do we regain balance?

My balance comes in the form of routine. When I was out in LA living on the street for those 37,440 minutes, the first few days were rough because I didn't have any balance, I didn't have a routine. Everything was all new to me.

Happy New Year!!!!!

As you can tell I've been on a bit of a hiatus from writing. It wasn't intentional, it just sort of happened. The most intriguing thing to me is how much this process has evolved. When I initially started to write this book, I was only going to make it about those 26 days I spent on the streets in LA. Then I noticed that I couldn't do that without giving a backstory. Then after that, I realized, I can't give a backstory without bringing the audience up to speed to what is currently happening in my life. From there, my initial intention was to utilize the last chapter of this book to inform the readers of what my current life is and how those 26 days impacted me. However, I think the process of writing this book is a fascinating experience that I want to share in real time. It's been therapeutic. This is my invitation to join me with not only the process of writing this book but the process of me revealing things about my life in the most vulnerable manner ever. Welcome to my book about me writing this book.

Here am I world.

These are the things that made me. It'll serve as a blueprint to see how these last 31 years were built. In return, all I ask is your patience and understanding. This isn't going to be your prototypical book. I'm not going to write chapters. This isn't going to be a technical piece of literary art. I'm ain't going to use perfect grammar. In fact, if you're into drinking games then taking a shot every time you see a grammatical or spelling error is sure enough to get the party started. Wait, on second thoughts, that might not end well because I'm sure there's going to bee a plethora fo mistakes form hear on out. To be responsible, I HIGHLY recommend that you do NOT take a shot for every mistake. Play it safe and take one for every 100 mistakes. That's sure to give you a nice buzz but remember to NOT drink and drive. Drink THEN drive. Thank me later. But as I was saying, before I rudely interrupted myself, this isn't going to be masterful in the forms that most people will expect. This will be masterful because it's something original. Nothing conceptual. Nothing pretentious. Nothing weighted. No propaganda. No bias. I'm going to tell you the best of the best about me and the worst of the worst about me. This is my manifestation. My intent is just to spark the minds of others. My intent is to share my experiences in hopes that some will relate and gravitate to my message and take something positive from it. My past led me to wanting to challenge myself at the age of 26 to live on the street. That decision impacted and changed my life tremendously. Hopefully getting to know me and my story with be impactful to others. Please read these words with an open mind and open heart. Now that I have your attention, allow me to bring you all up to speed.

Location: Chicago, IL
Date: January 15, 2016
Time: 7:02am

Ready? Ok, let's do this! On December 24th, I flew from LA to Dallas to meet my cousin who lives there. She picked me up from the airport and from there we drove to Houston to visit her mom and siblings. After Houston, I intended to leave Sunday, December 27th, and ride back to Atlanta with my friend who would be in Houston visiting her family also. After a few days in Atlanta, I planned to take the bus to Kentucky. Unfortunately, my friend got sick and never made the drive to Houston. No worries. Plan B was to stay in Houston for a couple of days with my aunt and have my sister mail my check that I had mailed to Kentucky mailed to my aunt's house. This was the most feasible option because I didn't have the funds to be able to make it to Kentucky, especially given the fact that it was New Year's. This is another reason I loathe holidays, all travel gets inflated. Minor issue. No biggie. Besides, those extra few days in H-town were welcomed because I love being with my family and hanging with the people I know there. Still following me? Fast forward to six days later. My check still hadn't arrived. My sister negated to put the Apt # on the address when mailing my check so it was never placed in my aunt's mailbox.

Not that it's relevant but I guess it should be explained why I had a check mailed to my parents house in Kentucky. When I was in LA, weeks before leaving on Christmas Eve, I worked as an extra on the show "Rosewood." Since I knew I'd be in Kentucky for the holidays, I had the check mailed to my parents house. Quick tidbit. Being on the set was a cool experience. We filmed a pool party scene which took a great level of acting because it was like 40 degrees that night but we had to give the impression that we were in Miami at a nice hotel pool party. Me and another extra, who was GORGEOUS by the way, were picked to portray a couple out enjoying a night on the town. Any excuse to spend time talking to a beautiful individual is fine by me. Add in the fact that I got paid for it and had access to free food made things all the more better for me.

Anyway, back to my broke a$$ and my everyday stalking of the mailbox. Being broke is amusing if you allow it to be. Being unexpectedly stranded in Houston for 10 days would be a tragic and a stressful experience for most people. For me, not so much. I'm fortunate that I was able to survive being there that long with approximately $20 bucks in my pocket. I'd be remissed if I didn't show an amazing amount of gratitude to my aunt, she was so incredibly gracious and hospitable. Thank you Aunt Bee!!! Love you!! The luxury of my lifestyle is that things really can't go wrong for me. Sure it was an unfortunate occasion but never once did I feel frantic. I didn't have to be at work on Monday, didn't have to rush home to my kids, didn't have anything I had to do or anywhere I had to be. My life was unfazed.

Ask me if I've received my check.

Gift, Have you received your check yet?

Nope.

Through the grace of Allah, he provided me with great friends and family who keep me from falling. Last Friday, I flew from Houston to Chicago. From Chicago I took the bus home to Kentucky. In the six days I was in Louisville, I went outside twice. Something about temperatures being in the teens that doesn't really motivate me to go outside. My intention of being in Louisville was to go there and work through this temp service I always use but the weather derailed those plans. One thing I learned in LA, is that give and ye shall receive. I'm not a person who holds on to money or tries to save henceforth why I'm routinely broke and why I was broke in every facet of the word for a solid 4 days last week. This isn't me just saying this to say this. I literally didn't have any money! I was the real, sincere authentic version of broke. Not the fake broke. There are some people who have money in their pocket but are "broke" in their minds because it's not enough to last them a certain amount of time. I don't have a savings account, heck I don't even have a bank account, so when I'm broke, I mean it in the most literally sense. As of yesterday, I literally didn't have a dime to my name. Literally. When I travel I never spend change. It was something I picked up from my dad growing up. He would keep jars of change and just cash them in when he needed cash. When I was in Houston, that's what I did. The change I had in my backpack totaled up to $11. So when I say I didn't have a dime, I literally mean it. Luckily, I received a charitable contribution from one of God's angels. So my eyebrows are above water now. As I was getting ready to take the bus here to Chicago, my dad, intrigued by my lifestyle, asked me:

> "How are you going to go out of town when you're broke?"

This is all just a work in progress.

This is my process.

Location: Los Angeles, CA
Date: April 7-8th, 2010
Day 3-4

One night of vulnerability bent me but didn't break me. After a few tears and deep sighs, at the crack of dawn, I found myself atop a parking structure in the Archlight Cinema complex located off Sunset Blvd. That view was something I grew to love. It brought me such peace and serenity. With my camera in hand I took in the panoramic view. On one side there was the skyline of downtown Los Angeles. To the far left you had the view of the Hills and the "Hollywood" sign. Behind me were the views of West Hollywood. It was an amazing vantage point to see the city in all it's glory especially the sight of palm trees, which warm my heart to see. It was so beautiful. Just to stand there and watch the sun ascend into the sky gave me perspective and a bit of confidence to get through this. This is what I wanted. This is where I wanted to be. While feeling seemingly atop the city I made the declaration to make the most of whatever came my way. To fight. To persevere. To not quit. To stay persistent. With my swagger and moral back on level 10, I felt like doing something to keep the ambiance and proverbial party going so I made my way to Goodwill to grab some new garb. With a vintage Levi Strauss denim jacket, vintage paper denim Guess jeans and a vintage hoody in hand, I walked out of there feeling great about life and what $20.73 allowed me to purchase. I spent the rest of the day walking around the Hollywood area and familiarizing myself with everything and getting a feel for things. Word to Osheal Jackson,

"Today was a good day."

Then the night fell.

My eventual nemesis throughout my pilgrimage became SLEEP. They say Death is undefeated. SLEEP is unblemished as well!. There is plausible cause for why it's said that "Sleep is the cousin of death." Sleep deprivation is like the most alarming feeling ever. It's a crazy feeling. It's almost like being near death because you lose control of your sense of self. It's like you're just drifting. Just floating as your mind starts to wander. It's hard to explain it but just imagine being sleepy and not being able to go sleep. Not insomnia. Not being restless. I'm saying not being able to go to sleep because you didn't have anywhere to sleep. Being forced to stay awake by your own paranoia that physically prevented you from sleeping. It's like slow torture. You have to fight off the urge to sleep. This came with the territory. It was something that I signed up for. The experience was something I wanted to stay genuine and true to while I was there. I didn't go there to be met with adversity then b*tch up and wimp out. This was welcomed adversity and it was my goal to conquer anything and fight all adversity to the death. This was my life on the line. This was my greatest life test and you don't learn by cheating so I had to endure the horrible outcomes. Everything takes time to get used to but I can tell you right now that I never got used to it. I never felt safe. I never felt comfort. I never felt completely at ease. It was a horrible thing to have to adjust to without any guidance. Without a plan and without any familiarity. I didn't know where to sleep or even where to go in order to sleep. I didn't feel confident enough to sleep outside because I didn't deem it safe. Unfortunately for me, I was reduced to adapting on the fly. That adaptation was learning not to sleep. Instead of sleeping, I simply walked around endlessly to quiet the exhaustion. I paid for it dearly as evident is this next clip that I transcribed for your reading pleasure:

> I am tired as H-E double hockey sticks. It's only um, I know it's 11 something, 11:41 on uh April 7th, a Wednesday, and I'm dead donkey tired yo, Like I just want to fall out right here. I got my vintage jeans on tho, you see me, balling, with my Levi Chucks, hurting my feet. I need some shoes, my feet are hurting too, Dangaw (inaudible) I was walking, I sat down and instantly I was sleepy, shouldn't of been walking. I cut on music, music ain't helping either, I just need to find somewhere, to get a quick nap in...
>
> ... Dang my finger hurt, don't you hate when like you cut your nail too short and I don't know, I don't know it got sore...
>
> ... ARRGGHH I'm sleepy...

(turns camera)

> *Peep the bench I'm on tho, bench, not b*tch. B-E-N. I thought it was about to say "2Pac" when I seen that "2" it should of said, it should, it should of said "2Pac... There go Borders..*
>
> *...Ahh but yeah, I'm tired, my ankle hurt, my feet hurt...*

> *The night time, I don't know, I thought it would be different, it feels a lot different, it feels a lot better, it's not as cold, but, when I get sleepy and I know I can't go nowhere and lay my head down that's like the, the kicker right there. Once I find me like a little uh place I know I can sleep in peace them imma be golden. The trouble is how can you sleep and go to peace when the world is around you? you got cars coming and going, I'd be too paranoid to sleep. But yeah I'm about to do something. One. U see me.*

Later that night.

> *Ok, so I just left uh the Donut Shop right there. (zooms camera towards establishment)*

> *that's where I did all my sleeping last night, but um there was a different guy in there today, I went in there trying to sneak some Zs in so I bought a donut to show uh good faith, and then, I didn't eat the donut because the donut was actually wack, and the place is dirty so I couldn't imagine eating in there, so you know what I'm saying, I had put my head on the table. probably like 10 minutes later, he wasn't banging on my table, he was banging where he was at like "no sleeping, no sleeping" I was like "aghh" so that uhhh threw a wrench in my gig, what I was about to do. Now, I don't know mane, about to go back over by the gym, ahh I'm so freaking tired tho!*

(Singing)

> *"know what to do, when it's coming to you"*

> *the gym is so wack man, if they had like longue chairs or something then I'd be straight. Their stuff is wack, they just got like benches, not even good ones, but yeah hold on... it's going on 1 O'clock, barely. Trying to see what I can get into, well sh*t where I can sleep to. I still need to..*

(noticing a woman on the bus stop bench)

> *dang she was out there last night, she just switched sides. that's weird that, when I zoom you can't see nobody*

> (focusing camera to be able to see her on camera)

> *you can see her now, well yeah she out holding that down.*
> (deep sigh)
> *Dang man, Dang! but um, yeah, We shall see...*

Few hours later.

> *So yeah the donut shop thing fell through and um, I mean, ain't no other options really. Lay down I suppose, and, I'm on, I'm just sitting on the bus stop I was on earlier, down the street from yao ming. but um, I ain't about to lay out but i'm about to do a quick, not a quick, but a hand to head thing catch some Zs, I fig, I mean it's not a bad spot, it's well lighted, cops riding by, I mean not, well cops may ride by but regular people riding by. but um, I ain't sleeping on the street but baby steps man, (laughs) I'm gone.. uh but yeah I'm going to leave the camera on the whole time tho, I don't know where I'm going to place it but it'll be on the whole time. so yeah, watch your boy.*

(Places camera down and proceeds to catch some Zs)

:14 Seconds later...

> Hold on, on second thought, it's in my hand clear as day, I don't want no junkie ride- walking past seeing my, seeing I got a camera in my hand.. so .. let me see if it'll fit in my jacket. nah ain't no hiding nothing. there go Tony Parker.

(Singing)

> "Street lights always, happen to be just like moments flashing..."

> I been doing too much walking man, I said I need to buy some Dr scholls I don't even know where to get them at

(long pause)

> Man...

> This is crazy...

Location: Atlanta, GA
Date: January 27,2016
Time: 8:50am EST

"There's nothing like a nice heaux bath at the airport to really get your day started and make you feel refreshed, motivated and creative enough to dive back into this book you're writing."

That was the sentiment and the words I spoke to myself as I exited the Men's restroom at Hartsfield-Jackson airport this morning. From the airport I hopped the train and arrived at my office, or Barn and Noodles as others refer to it, here on 5th and Spring St prepared for greatness. I'm clocked in and ready to work to convey my life story for your literary pleasure.

When we left off, I was in Chicago. That same day, I flew into the DMV area. I spent January 16th-20th there before flying here to Atlanta. While in the DMV I spent time with one of "my lovely's, my dime" as Denzel's character in Tanning Day would say. More about her later. Well no, not later. Why wait? I'll inform you all of her now. It's soooo COMFORTING and awesome how certain people end up in each other lives almost at the perfect time. It's great to have somebody in your corner and in turn you're in their corner to help them grow as they help you to grow. Especially at a moment in time when both people are going through changes and dealing with adversity. Nobody likes to be alone so I value and cherish the genuine bonds, relationships and friendships I'm allowed to foster in this journey we call life. Thank you for being YOU and from everything within me, I'll always value, cherish and appreciate you for being there for me and making this journey not as horrendous as it could have been. All love.

Good news everybody.

MY CHECK FINALLY CAME!!!! BALLING!!!!!!

While in Chicago, I called the casting agency in LA to have them reissue me another check and mail it to Louisville. Now comes the task of having it mailed here to my cousin's house. I'm eager to cash it and literally spend the whole check paying back the people I had to borrow money from since my broke a$$ has been without it for a month. Isn't that how life goes sometimes? You can't even be excited about a check because you know as soon as you cash it it'll be all gone. What a buzz kill. More money. More debt.

For as long as I can remember, one of my sources of motivation has been people telling me what I can't or shouldn't do. It's something in me that likes to be defiant. Proving people wrong is another one my passions. I live for it. I love to do things to push myself. A few years ago, I fell in love with running. Growing up, running was always punishment, especially for those of us who played organized sports. I'm not sure why I started running but I started off just doing 20 minute runs around my sister Lorna's neighborhood when I came to visit her here for almost a month back in 2009-ish. It started with me only doing a mile or two mile each time. Now I'm in peak physical condition and can run 10 miles easily. Running is a constant challenge but a rewarding challenge. It's more mental than physical for me because you have to be mentally tough to push yourself. There has been times when I was running and physically felt like stopping. Last January, I partnered up with a buddy of mine from middle school who reached out to me on Face and the book because he too shared a passion for running as well. I used to post my runs on Face and a Book and people took notice to that. They would reach out to me to share their love for running. Due to this, my buddy reached out and we developed a business relationship. He owns a performance apparel company called "Run Baby Run" well now it's called "RBR active". I was tasked with creating and executing marketing and branding campaigns as well social media promotions. One of the great things about his company is that it's philanthropically based. His focus isn't primarily based on profits for gain. His emphasis is having more in order to be able to do more. Using profits to give back and create opportunities for others. We were essentially promoting positive living and using running as the conduit. In doing the company branding, I came of with a slogan to really drive home our brand initiative:

"Life is a race, stay on track"

Running is comparable with how life is. It's challenging. It's hard. It takes time and commitment. Focus. Dedication. Often times you want to stop but you can't stop. You can't quit. You can't give up. See it to the end. Finishing is rewarding because through adversity you learn and grow.

"Struggle builds success"

Throughout life we'll be faced with hard times adversity and challenges. I love challenges. The more the better. My brother, LaVon inadvertently challenged me when I was home in the 502 a few weeks ago. He brought up the fact that I'm approaching 32 and in not so many words, that it might be time to settle down. It was his way of more or less saying "Stop wasting your talent and go be somebody." He felt I needed some form of stability. He said it lovingly but as I told him, I took that as a personal challenge.

The "stability" that my brother may have been referring to is that form of stability of staying in one place, having a house, a car or a career isn't a bad thing. Me and my lovely had a similar discussion on the topic. What I explained in a conversation with her was that being "stable" means consistent. The "standard" and ideal of "stability" is to have a house, a car and job. Three things I don't have. As I alluded to earlier, traveling is my structure and form of stability. All I do is travel. Consistently. When people text me, they often ask what city I'm in. So much so that one person now refers to me as "Carlton San Diego." That's my form of stability, I feel stable in what others deem unstable. I'm 31. Yes. But I've been living on my own since I was 18. I've been providing for myself since I was cutting grass with my uncle and granddad as early as the age of 9. There's that blank space and gap of my life that people aren't privy to. People just assume that I've never had anything, never did anything and that my lifestyle is a result of a failure and don't realize that it's a choice. I love to travel. Amongst the people I've come in contact with, they develop some weird assumptions based on my lifestyle. One odd thing that people ask is if I know how to drive. Apparently, not having a car means you don't have a car and it's believable that in my life I've never owned one or ever learned to drive. Laugh Out Loud. Not having a house, apartment or place of my own gives people the assumption that I've never had one, that I've never paid rent and that it's believable that I don't know what it's like to have anything of my own. Laughing My A$$ Off. The main thing people ask and come up with theories about is how I generate money to be able to afford to pay for flights. Apparently, I'm either a male escort, have rich parents, involved in some scam or have a sugar moma. Rolling On The Floor Laughing. It seems to be a habit that people formulate opinions based on negativity and skepticism. If something is unheard of or not plausible to them in their mind, then there has to be some sinister reasoning behind my lifestyle and other people's lifestyle. None of those assumptions are accurate. I travel simply because I love to travel!!! I'm homeless because I enjoy the freedom of not being tied to anything which means I can travel as often as possible. These are sacrifices that I'm consciously making. These aren't decisions I'm making out of necessity or circumstances. I'm making sacrifices to get what I want done. The past two nights I slept at the airport.

Why?

Because I wanted to.

Why would I want to?

Because I wanted to.

Makes sense?

No?

Good.

Today is Wednesday, I've had the same thing on since Monday.

Why?

Because I wanted to.

Because I had to?

Nope.

Make sense?

No?

Good.

Let me explain:

Last night I met up with a friend of mine named Irene. We sat and had discussions on life and all things that matter. She shared her desire to break out of this "box" she felt she was in. She's been slowly peeling back the layers to her life to gain additional knowledge and understanding. She texted me after I left and told me I made her day. That's right people. I'm out here making people's day! How did I make her day you ask? Was it because I gave her a new car? No. Was it because I did her a huge favor? No. It was because of my presence. It was because I take time to listen to people. It's because I take time to talk to people. It's because I take time to invest in getting to know people for who they are and not who I want them to be. That's why I don't apologize for sh*t. My life's purpose is loud and clear to me. It's not to appease people by the car I drive, the clothes I wear, my credit score or where I live. Just seeing her smile and see her let her guard down was beautiful. Her goal is to become fearless. She wants to really put herself out there and go for the things she really wants. She conveyed how she had an awakening. She felt like she had been lied to and that this perception and narrative of what life is was able to steal her identify. Sound familiar? She had reached a point where she has settled for working at a job that doesn't fulfill her. That same thing is true for a lot of people. It's my greatest belief that you should do whatever makes you happy. You shouldn't compromise that.

Speaking of what makes you happy, feeling like I'm always in the right place at the right time makes me happy. The day after I landed in Atlanta, I saw a casting post on Face and the book about doing background work on a feature film here. It was something I could do so I submitted and got booked to work Friday, January 21st and yesterday. The movie takes place in the 90s so when I arrived on set they gave me a 90s haircut and dressed me like a R&B thug. To compliment my baggy jeans, versace-esque dress shirt, leather vest and Jodeci boots, they decided that it'd be a amazing idea to shave my beard and leave me with just a pedophile-esque mustache. It was amusing to me so I sent a picture to my siblings. LaVon texted me to express that he was supremely proud and just happy that his kid brother was on a movie set! He then proceeded to post the picture on Face and the book while gleaming with pride and informing people I was on the set of this major movie. September 27th, 2015 was my last day utilizing social media. I posted a farewell message because as I found out during my last social media hiatus that if you don't post online for a while, people assume that you're dead. Due to the fact I'm writing a book right now, wait, Did I mention that I'm writing a book? Well if I haven't, then I apologize but I'm currently writing a book and decided that I needed to maintain my creativity and not spend it with mindless dribble that goes on on tweeter, face and the book, or instagrahm. That being said, somehow the picture Von posted on his page posted to my page as well. Immediately I began to get congratulatory text messages. Not one for unwarranted attention, I urged him to remove the post from his page. He heeds my wishes. Only to post it back up! It was at like 60 likes by then. I joked with him that he was using me for "likes".

What my brother failed to mention was that I'm on set working as a background extra and went through wardrobe both days but never made it past holding. Which means I never made it on set to actually do any filming. His post alluded to that fact that I was acting and on set of a major movie and I never made it to set. See how this could be misleading? The picture I took was when I was still in wardrobe. That isn't anything for people to be happy or proud of but as my brother told me, to people working a dead end 9-5 job, being on movie set of a big movie is enough to be happy about. For me, it's business as usual. Nobody knows the people I've been in the same room with. The relationships I've built with influential people because to me it's no big deal. It's not my instinct to try to glorify it and say "Hey look at me, I'm cool" Never has it even entered my mind to get pictures with this person or take pictures of being in these places so that I can post it online. Wait. That's a lie. The first and ONLY time I ever asked for a picture was when I met Big Boi from Outkast at his charity event. I asked for a picture, he agreed but as soon as I saw the picture I told the person who took it to delete it. I've never had a platinum album but he's no different or better than me so why should I be in awe of another human? If you're constantly looking up to people when will you find time to look up to yourself? Nothing wrong with appreciating another person's talent and ability but no need to glorify them. They're people too.

This generation is consumed with being attached to something to paint themselves as something substantial. Like I told my brother, I don't want that, I don't care about trying to be somebody. I care about being somebody who can spend time having a conversation with a person and be there to offer advice and feedback as she is sharing with me her vulnerability and how talking in front of people makes her nervous then confide in me how she has hopes to become a motivational speaker and life coach. As Irene and I set in her living room, I encouraged her to start her Yourtube page that she had an idea for but hadn't done yet. Helping her set it up, giving her pep talks, instigating her to let her guard down, press record and post the short introduction video for her Vlog about her journey to being fearless is what matters to me.

All day yesterday I received these well wishes and celebratory praises from people I haven't heard from in years. This only made me more spiteful and feel validated for why I shy away from being or having anything. It's not genuine. People see you as "Doing big things now" and then they want to reach out to you. That annoys my soul. Those same people are the same ones who'll question what I'm doing in my life. If I was to tell people where I've been and what I've done then it'll kill all their naive superficial perceptions. In part, I guess, that's what this book is, huh?

Here I am.

This is a guy who's more comfortable sleeping at the airport if I feel it's more convenient for me and because it's less of a hassle. The night before last I slept at the airport because there was an early call time and instead of staying somewhere and having to wake up early and figure out how to get to set on time. I decided to stay at the airport and catch the train early and use an Vber free ride promo code to get from the train station to set. When I left Irene's house last night it was fairly late. Instead of taking the train, then the bus to my cousin's house and have to wake her up in order for her to let me in the gate, I choose to just go sleep at the airport. I could of went other places but I didn't because not going was more convenient. I'd rather not have to have people fit me into their schedule if I can get around it.

This is me.

This is a guy who cares more about others at times more than he cares about himself. This is a guy who has $15 bucks to his name as he types these words. Last night at the airport, I was woken up by a lady tapping my leg asking for a dollar. I said no initially, then laid back down. I opened my eyes and seen her looking in her backpack for change so I reached in my wallet and handed her a dollar. There was a guy on the other side of the bench I was laying on and I'm guessing he saw my gesture because he reached over the seats and handed her a dollar as well. Afterwards she looked at me and said "God bless you" then went and bought some food.

This is me.

This is a guy who understands his life purpose and that exchange last night at the airport was apart of that. This is a guy who wants to represent something great in humanity and society in hopes that others adapt the same good will and pass it on to others so that it snowballs. This is a guy who wishes that as a society the emphasis isn't put on shedding light on all the negatives but instead allowing positivity to shine. It seems like the focus is more often placed on the differences between things than it is placed on the similarities. It's like you constantly have to pick sides. You constantly have to be one thing or another. They want you to fit into a box. They want to control you. They want to dictate your happiness and freedom. They want to manipulate you. They want to perpetuate fear to limit you. They display negative images thoughts and ideas to show you the possible repercussions. They want you to be scared of the water. They don't want you to get in that boat. They don't want you to succeed. They don't want you to go against the grain. They don't want you to live your life. I say F*ck they. They won't be there in your dark times. They won't be there when it counts. They won't be there when it matters. They don't matter. This is your life. You own you. Don't give up ownership of your identity. don't give up ownership of your goals. Don't give up ownership of your dreams. Don't give up ownership of your life. It's yours.

It took me 1 day 24 hours and 34,560 minutes to finally realize this.

This is crazy...

Location: Los Angeles, CA
Date: April 8th, 2010
Day 4

(Camera pans to show the outside)

> ... As yall can see, it's morning again, well becoming morning...

> ...Um last night um, after I left the donut spot, I went to the gym and um, tried to sleep in there and was told told "no sleeping" "no sleeping" "no sleeping."...

> ...so, hmmm, I probably logged about 45 minutes all night, I say 15 at the donut spot then 30 at the gym. uh It's 6:18am right now, uh, I got woke up at the gym around 4, 4 and some change. I was just in there, ya know, tweetin and textin then I went and uh took a shower, soaked my uh feet in the, in the hot tub, then came here for some breakfast but...

> ... I ordered a sausage biscuit right? like eh, just get me a, Imma take it light, I don't want to spend a bunch of money on breakfast because it is early and I'm going to eat at least two more times today, but then I said, breakfast is the most important part of the day, so why not get breakfast? so I got breakfast. I said let me, let me get that breakfast deluxe shawty...

(turns camera to show food on table)

> ...and this is what I unveiled, after um, the pancakes were cold, this, this is hard, bread is hard, hard, look at these eggs, eggs look like rubber, see this shiny sh*t? looks like rubber, I never eat the hashbrowns but yeah this was $5.30...

(drops camera)

Fumble.

(picks camera up)

>   ...I paid $5.30 for that to sit on a plate, um you would think a somebody being homeless would have more um, um what you call it? desperateness? desperateness? but nah I just be wasting food. I should've just got the sausage biscuit, I'm tryna, ya know make up for last night because I didn't get any sleep, so I'm like I'mma treat myself and I ended up tricking myself. but yeah, I'm bout be in here for the foreseeable future, I ain't got nowhere to go to and nothing to do. ain't no point of, point of walking around, my feet still hurt. so yeah, I think my personal best is like 5 hours. back when uh, back In college, I waited 5 hours, inside mcdonald's, just chilling, cause I was waiting, I was trying to get a ride somewhere. back when Jimmy was working there, I waited like 5 hours...
>
>   ... Today um, I probably, probably could do 5 hours, we'll see. now it's April 8th, 6:21am. and um we'll check back in um 5 hours. (laughs) You See Me.

(Later that day)

>   ...yeah just uh, left out of the library over there...

(pans camera back towards library)

>   ...I was in there for a good what, two almost three hours got a lot, lot of nice little sleep..

(turns camera back to POV and starts walking down the street)

...what I'm learning, see them people right there on the step? oh you can't see'em

(turns camera towards library and people in front)

...dude right there, people over there. what I'm learning is, I don't know If they're all homeless but they all know each other. I don't know if they like, I don't know, it's weird because I see the same people together like, like from Popeyes, like, the same people from there, was in the library just now, so it's like weird. I don't know, it's like some little, community, they all know each other, but yeah um, got some great sleep in there, uh I feel sick my throat, um, my throat is all aggy. I said I'm about to go see if I can find some ice cream somewhere, but yeah, if I get sick, that's gone ugh, that's gonna add insult to injury. so yeah, I'm trying to find some ice cream, I don't even know why I came this way, ahhh.. man, ain't no restaurants on here. I'm think i'm just gone head uh, gone head go to Mcdonalds. it's weird just, I'm trying like to add some like structure like some routine not routine just something, I know I can do just trying to plan my days so I have something to do, since I'm just always wandering around, all this walking is for the birds. cause my uh...

...oh, I think it's bad to luck to go through these things (under a scaffold), I slipped up and went to it that time, but, never again...

...a toilet?...

...it feels good outside tho, feels real good. think it's like 80 or something...

... yeah my, my achilles is hurting like a mug...

...damn, she looks good up there...

... but yeah I'm on a quest to get some ice cream for my throat, you see me, one...

(hours later)

...so yeah, I'm still, um I was about to say Burger King but I'm still at Mcdonald's, had my ice cream, it was alright,but wasn't all that, my throat still hurting, and I think, I'm hot...

...I feel hot...

...I feel um, drained...

...yeah I feel drained, I have no energy...

...I was about to go to um, Rite Aide and get some cough syrup, not cough syrup, cough drops. Clearly I didn't make it. I got up, went to the bathroom, then sat right back down...

...but yeah um day what? 3? 4?...

...dah di duh dah...

...I never knew I could feel so lazy in life, it's pathetic...

...I was thinking like, I don't even know how I got over here...

...I don't remember, I don't remember, I don't remember the walk from like to get here from the library, to get here, I just popped up here, I think I um teleported or something...

...I been uh...

(turns camera towards face)

...like this for like, 40 minutes...

(sitting with elbow on table, handle on side of face and shoulder leaning against the wall)

...no bueno...

...but yeah, um, next stop? I don't know I'll probably be in here, uhh I'm just not feeling it...

...Help me Tom Cruise.

Location: Atlanta,GA
Date: January 31, 2016

Good day folks. It occurred to me yesterday that I stopped using Chapter titles. I've just been writing continuously. I wonder if for book purposes that you have to have chapters. The index will be hard to make but who really needs an index? It's probably best just to treat this as a diary. Initially, I was writing it as a book, as evident of how amazing the first few pages were written. This is more my speed tho, I'm not trying to make people over think or get too creative. I just want to share my unique experiences with the world. This process has been so fulfilling and had it not been for Zey, I would of not even thought to do this. Thanks ZEY!!!!!!

It's been fascinating to go through this process. My initial goal was to have 26 chapters and write a chapter about each day I was there. That morphed into my having an idea to start every chapter with a poem to correlate with the chapter titles. There were like 10 or so chapter titles that I had came up with and planned to write in correlation to what I went through in LA. That obviously didn't go as planned but maybe I'll periodically write poems when I do my journal entries and updates. It's kind of like I really writing a book about writing a book. Often times I think to myself, "What would Jerry do?" *Seinfeld* was one of my favorite shows growing up (second only to *Fresh Prince of Bel Air.*) Writing this book reminds me of how *Seinfeld* was conceptually "The show about nothing" This is the "book about nothing" but it's about everything. The irony.

Yesterday, and part of today, was spent working on set of that movie I was working on the other day and I actually made it to SET!!! MOMA I MADE IT!!!!! That was the first movie set I had EVER been on so it was a cool process. I played it cool but it was a big deal to me. The first two days I never made it to set so I felt cheated but yesterday I finally made it to set. Not only did I make it to set; I was all in the camera, all in the scene, pantomiming, walking. reacting to dialogue. If there was a Oscar category for background acting then I'd be shoe in. I'm not sure how the editing will shake out but if you watch that *All Eyez On ME* Tupac movie just know I'm speckled in there in a few different scenes. Today, we got sent home early because they overbooked so I figured I'd come to my office and keep this book progressing. Back in October-ish, 2015-ish, I told myself that I would take off the entire month to write this book. According to my watch, it's February and I'm not sure if I'm even half done yet.

...Help me Tom Cruise.

Location: Los Angeles, CA
Date: April 9th, 2010
Time: 3:31am
Day 5

      So yeah, it's Friday April the 9th, 3:31am. As you can see I'm on top of a rooftop, you know what I'm saying just chilling, not chilling, just doing nothing basically but um yeah I just wanted to see the city...

      ... then I got a bright idea, was like, you seen, yall seen "Hangover" right? figured I might pull a Doug you feel me, the white Doug not the black Doug and catch some z's on the rooftop. I probably, only need not too many, too much time, just need like a little nap...

      ...or just wait until somebody get me, come get me. I don't think it's illegal to sleep on a roof is it? probably just tell me to take my dumb ass on somewhere. Hope not, ain't no, hope nobody pissed over here...

      ...yeah, they got the camera's over there, on that pole...

      ...got a bogey on the roof..

(lays down on ground)

      ...aghhh..

(pans camera around rooftop and zooms in)

      ...there goes the W...

      ...something...

      ...ah this ground is hard...

... but yeah, I'mma leave the camera on, I ain't going to be able to hold it but let me see what I can do with it...

(props camera)

...I don't know...

...wonder how much battery I got...

(Looks at playback screen)

...don't nobody want to see that, just a camera posted up...

...but yeah, today was probably like um my best day here, know I'm saying, it was uh, you know I'm saying, every hour was accounted for, know I'm saying, um went uh Mcdonalds this morning, around five or six, stayed in there til like 9, what, um what I do again? yeah, I went to there, stayed about 9, nah, dang, it had to be earlier than that. I went in there like 5 or 6 and stayed til like 8. and then, what I did? is that when I went and got ice cream? yeah, I think that's when I went and got ice cream and then I went to the library and then I went back to Mcdonald's? I was in Mcdonalds basically all day. It's good because they didn't put me out or tell me I couldn't sleep. and then uh I went to the gym, nah, I went to the gym, and I went um washed laundry and now I'm on the rooftop. Wish I had a blanket...

...that's all I want...

but yeah, this probably the best day so far. I had like, Usually at night time when I'm walking around I get sleepy like man where am I going to sleep at? ARRGG GRRR! that's like the uh the uh downfall so to speak like man, what am I doing? but tonight, I, I went for little walk until my feet started hurting like man let me cut this short but at no point was I, was I, did I get frustrated. I'm pretty much uh well rested, but yeah man, on the roof top. I need, I'm sleepy but, I ain't as sleepy as I have been. I swear it feels like I've been here for weeks. This is only what, Monday, Tuesday, Wednesday Thursday. I've only been here for 4 days, well not even 4 days because Monday I didn't get here til like 9 or at something at night. So just say Tuesday, Wednesday and Today so like 3 whole days...

...Today was good, I'mma do everyday like I did today. Tomorrow, I think I''m um, I'mma go find other gyms, know I'm sayin, hopefully they not, I don't know. they ain't too far away, I just want to see what they like, just to see a different part of town, tired of seeing this, feel me?

...I just seen a headlight...

...they coming to get me already?...

...I thought I saw a headlight, yeah...

(singing)

"Dream of Californication..."

yeah once soon as I get my feet under me and get used to this sleeping arrangement or lack thereof then I'll start making my sign and doing all that stuff, yeah, but yeah this is good for now, um, if I get woke up or wake up again I'll go, I was about to say go live like I'm on "Ustream." If I wake up again, I'll film it, for now, signing off folks, April 9th, 3:37 in the morning chicka chicka oww. You see me.

(1 hour later)

(stretching as I yawn)

...well, I did my little uh, hold on, I think it was like 3 something, hour, hour and a half, probably like a hour, hour and a half.

(pulls phone out to check the time)

(laughing)

...not even that, just a hour. aw welp, man...

...aw man...

...felt like forever...

...there goes my uh, my initiation, my gold star for sleeping outside, agh it's cold if I had a blanket I would of still been sleep...

...jacket all dirty..

...now I'm about to go in here, hot tub my feet, then um start the day...

...alright, you see me. One.

Let me add some context and commentary for you all right now. The gym in question that I frequented was attached to the parking structure I slept on the rooftop of. It's the place where I mentioned seeing my first sunrise. I went up there that night just to see the city. There's not a lot of traffic up there especially at 3am. There was this dark spot along a concrete slab in the far end of parking lot. When I was up there I noticed it and thought it'd be a nice place to lay down because I wouldn't have to worry about strangers walking past or cars driving by or anything. It was a remote location so on that night I FINALLY built up the gusto to get further out my comfort zone and lay down. When you've essentially been up for like 3 days, you get desperate. I most certainly was desperate. I wanted sleep. I wanted to feel relaxed.

That hour felt like forever. Unlike sleeping it Mcdowells or the library, I didn't wake up every so often just to look around and make sure my belongings were there or not let myself get too far into sleep. That night I let go. It was calming. Walking had been my combat for fighting sleep but what I didn't know at the time was that when I don't sleep properly or when I'm not able to elevate my feet then my feet, along with my lower legs, become swollen. It still happens to me. My friend, who is a nurse, whom I told of my symptoms told me what I could attribute it to the name escapes me but it's something "atrophy" which just means poor circulation and fluid buildup. It's caused by lack of sleep and something about motion.

DO NOT EAT THE FIBER BARS!!!!!

Ok. I'm back, don't worry, I courtesy flushed. Have you ever used the handicapped stall and felt guilty? I used to do it all the time. It's so roomy. Today, I decided not to for fear that out of all days today would be the day I'd be in there and just my luck a handicapped person would come in trying to use it. Then I'd have to deal with the glares and evil eyes as I walked out of there to see them. In all my years of public restrooms, I have never seen a handicap person using that stall. Thanks to the law of averages I always take the chance. Today I guess I became paranoid Anywho.

Have you ever been working on writing a book and in your mind continue to work to come to a good stopping point because they're gas bubbles going off in your stomach like 4th of July and are giving indications that Its. About. To Go. Down. In. A. Major. Way. TMI? I'm sure, but as I said this has turned into a diary and journal and what's a journal without sharing how eating 10 Fiber One bars within the last two days on set wasn't a good idea? Right? Welp that's a good enough stopping point. Nature is calling.

Let's set the scene:

.

I'm back in LA and the unthinkable is about to happen. Dun. Dun. Dun. Dun. DUUUUUNNNNNNNNN. This was my first true test of being alone in a place I don't live and had never been. This was the night things really became apparent how far I was away from home and how far I was away from comfort.

...alright, you see me. One.

Location: Los Angeles, CA
Date: April 9th, 2010
Time: 11:42pm
Day 5

...um...

...bad news guys, um...

...terrible bad news...

...um, apparently, let me show you the sign...

(camera turns and zooms in on sign)

...it says, it says "24 Hr Fitness" but apparently there's some small fine print that says on friday nights that the door closes at 11:30 and this was unbeknownst to me, obviously, so it is, un momento, it is, where my phone at? it is 11:42 so I was making, I was mosing up to, ya know, the fitness place tryna do my thing, get, kill some time take a nap or something, and then I noticed, um a sign on the door that says um Gym closes at 11, no, door closes at 11, gym closes at 1130. I read it like 10 times just to make sure I got it right, and yeah I did. It was not good, so ummm yeah. I'm really, I don't know what I'mma do. I don't know when they gon open it back up. all my stuff is there. ummm, so yeah, more than likely um I'll be sleeping on the street tonight, don't know where, don't know how but uh when push comes to shove, uh you gotta do what gotta do what you have to do. It's crazy cause man, I ain't gonna even say it but urrggghh, I think, I don't know, how you, some, I got jinxed. I got jinxed, jinxed and hours later, look what happened. I'm just going to rely on my sheer positivity and optimism right now but on the inside, on the inside of me I am livid, I am spazzing, spazzing, on the inside, but on the outside I'm pretending that it ain't nothing...

...but um, what the heck hell am I gonna do?...

...this wasn't part of the plan, I didn't sign up for this...

...arrggghh...

...I ain't mean to cuss, my foot hurt, I know I'm going to be sleepy man...

...huugghh...

...I don't even know, but yeah it's thick outside tho, maybe I'll find me a nice young lady to, nah, well alright, I'll check back when something happens...

(1 hour later)

April 10, 2010
Day 6

so yeah I'm just walking man, I was trying to cool off ,but hey man at the end of the day, once it happens it's done, know I'm saying? ain't nothing I can do about it. but adapt and ya know, make the most of it, somehow, someway. I don't know what that is yet but um I'm here still, so that's enough to build upon, yeah, so either love me or leave me alone.

(hours later)

so yeah um, back at it, posted, sitting on the corner of um Yucca and something, you see the Knickerbocker, Capitol records some more bullshit over here, but yeah I think i'm gon um chill out man.....think i'm just going to chill out as I see it, Mcdonalds open in a few hours man so, man I had the option of ya know I could of eradicated the matter ya understand but that was two hours ago man.

I'm off that. but yeah my feet hurt, I think I done tore some, my ankle man, think I done tore some ligaments in that thing again. ain't no sense for it to be hurting uh this long. aw but yeah, I ain't going to be sitting right here forever but it's a nice rest up spot. yeah...

(Singing)

"such is life, such is life."

ummm, I wish my, see, I wish my, my foot and stuff wasn't messed up, I would make fun of this and like do some like just walk around all night just being random. I don't know, I don't think my battery would last too long but it's a journey just to walk how far I walked. but yeah we'll see how it goes man. I'll check back or something. get with your boy man. you see me...

(roughly 45 mins later)

...this expressway up here, it's uh 1:01 just walking to the store, dang I need some better lighting it's like 1,2,3,4,5,6,7 people under the bridge, then some more over here. I figured this is where you could find some of them at...

...they bundled up nicely...

....them is people man, just look like, look like dead bodies...

...but yeah um I'm about to go to the store real quick and get some snacks, some fat snacks, cause ya know I need my sugar, ya feel me. but yeah um, I gotta cross the street, don't hit me, don't hit me. aw can't even run my ankle man, sheesh...

...oh wow, damn, I see you in that Camry, y'all see her? biem, biem, yeah that's it, she got a friend with her too, her friend wack tho. about to get me some snacks...

(1 hour later)

...just been, I ended up walking, walking up and down Hollywood Boulevard for like a hour, it was dumb thick out there, looking like Derby minus the rims and all black people but it was thick man. I saw some um, a couple dudes got debo'd, it was, ya know i'm sayin, I guess that's what happens down here. It was alright tho, whole bunch of white chicks, it was some cute black chicks but for the most it was snowbunnies...

...now I got what? um, hold on, let me see what time it is, hold on, it's 2:41 so I probably got what two hours to kill, so all I know is I gotta pee, that's gonna be the first thing I do is go to the bathroom and then, then go from there. uhhhhhhh you see me! gone, gone, gone, gone you see me, gone.

(8 hours after being locked out of gym)

...Moma I made it, as you can tell, I'm in my favorite place. Eight hours later, I walked a good, probably like 5 or 10 miles altogether, distance between walking back, back and walking back and forth down the strip and whatever. I set out to (clears throat) excuse me, I set out to do it and I did it. I ain't get no sleep, just been out in these streets son, feel me? cause I do that. you know you sleepy when you fall asleep eating. I was eating my Mcflurry, I mean my sundae and next thing I know I was sleep. I'm about to fall asleep right now matter fact eating this, umm cinnamon melt, I used to kill these all the time when I worked at Mcdonalds, that's all I ate but yeah, I ain't got no um, couldn't charge my phone, I got like a bar left, but shoot *ain't nobody up right now no way, I don't need it, bout to take this nap and call it a day homie, but yeah man, I made it...*

(Singing)

"we made it, looks like we made it..."

...how does that song go?..

(singing)

"we made it..."

aw dang man my eyes are going ham, they're like ay man, put us down, we tryna we tryna relax but yeah, I'm bout to go to sleep...

(lays head on table)

... yall be good. thanks for having me, Gift, you see me.

That night was the night that gave me the feeling of:

"Hey, I can do this."

After having breakfast I took the bus to UCLA to watch CRod's track meet. I had known CRod for years. We met via a mutual friend on Face and the Book. Back around this time, I had a side hustle of making graphic tees. C-Rod would always post pics after her workouts with the caption "Fresh Out of Practice." Me seeing this, after taking a liking to her, I designed a shirt for her with that phrase on it and sent it to her. She loved it. We became cordial friends and kept in touch over the years. When I got out to California I went to show my support. The really amazing thing was that at this event, CRod just so happened to be running relays with the future mother of my kids, Alyson Felix. It was another paradox to my situation. Here I was living on the streets while still taking time to do cool stuff. It's not everyday people have friends or know people who just competed in the Olympics. It's kind of symbolic that with my life, I'm not far removed from the things I aspire to be or the things I aspire to do. For this reason, I feel as if I can sacrifice for a higher purpose. There isn't any what ifs or maybes to my life. I'm comfortable and confident with who I am as a person. The phrase lemons to lemonade comes to mind. Living on the streets became casual to me because I made it casual. I didn't allow my circumstances to defeat me. Don't get me wrong, there were a ton of rough times but rough times make you appreciate the not so rough times. I welcomed it all. I appreciated it all. I appreciated the little things. Little things like taking time to sit on a bench outside of UCLA's campus in Bel-Air and take a photo. For me that moment was special because coming from Kentucky we never see luxury cars or million dollar houses in such abundance. We'd see these things on TV but never even fathomed the thought of these things actually existing in real life. Sometimes you have to pretend. That's the best escape from unfortunate situations. Being the Fresh Prince of Bel-Air for even a moment was enough for me.

What I've learned is, the more you go through, the more you can make it through. Being stranded out all night isn't something that's common and for good reason. Most people would have had a hard time trying to make it through the night. I made it through. Being hungry, I made it through that. Being scared, I made it through that. Being home sick, I made it through that. This is my journey and what I subjected myself to. There are people who went through way worse. Those battling illnesses. Those dealing with the loss of a close one. The list goes on. My experience pales in comparison to those things. To some degree I can keep things in perspective. I was fortunate. My experience forced me to adapt. It forced me to fight. Forced me to not give up. Nobody was going to come to rescue me or save me. There was nowhere for me to go to escape anything and I purposely made it that way.

There's nothing I can type to express or properly detail how somber, sad and vulnerable all the words I've shared and will share throughout this process are. Being there I learned to not complain. I learned to tolerate things. It wasn't something I learned from day one but as the process went on, I grew as a person. I learned how to maintain during a stressful and unfortunate situation. You guys have NO idea just how rough those first few days were. There was no familiarity. Nothing safe. No comfort. No solace. There was a constant need to always be aware of my surroundings. It got to a point where I developed a habit of looking behind me every 3-5 seconds. This experience was like a trial by fire scenario. There wasn't anything to guide me other than faith. So that's what I followed. What I trusted. What I believed in. When I was home most recently I had a conversation with my dad and I was explaining to him why I decided to take this journey. It made me think of the quote "Walk by faith and not by sight" That's why I did,I put my faith and trust in a higher power. It's cute and cool to say it but how can you show you mean it? This wasn't me walking into a church and walking to an altar and telling a pastor I'm giving myself to God. This was me talking with God and telling God, I'm giving you my life. "In thee I put my faith, all my battles he will fight" My spirituality didn't come from a book, didn't come from a sermon. It came from real life. The fact that I tried to kill myself multiple times is a REAL thing. I lost my desire and will to live. Being unsuccessful in my attempts made me realize I'm supposed to be here. It was up to me to figure out why. It took me years of going through the motions until one day I made the revelation. I said to myself *"This isn't your life. This isn't for you."*

Oh snap, I just remembered that I emailed TT something when I was 24 about how I had this eerie feeling about how I felt like I was going to die when I was 25. Let me see if I can find that email. I told her not to read it until after I died.

Story developing...

No luck. I don't even know what email I even used at that time but I texted TT and asked her to check her email and search my names to see if she comes across anything like that. I vaguely remember it. I know it was related around my death. Not sure if it was a suicide note but what I do remember is that for a while I had this instinct and this feeling that I was going to die at the age of 25. Don't ask me why. It was a strong intuition. In my mind, I was just waiting for it to happen. I was waiting for that year to come so I could just die. The email I sent to TT could've been me telling her that. At any rate, this all ties into what I was saying about me realizing that at 25 working as a cashier wasn't the life that I was meant to be living. Hindsight is fascinating. Your life is exactly how it is meant to be. Everything you go through, the decisions you make, dictate what goes on in your life. Moving to Atlanta was meant to get the proverbial ball rolling in regards to reaching my destiny and finding my life purpose.

I Fell in Love In Atlanta
April 5, 2009

Now off top I could type this describin how great she is
how she make me feel and that she is oh so pretty
lead u on the whole time and then at the end come up with somethin witty
and then reveal that the whole time I wasn't talkin about a girl but instead a city
yea that was one option but imma take the 2nd, cause that's the day i was born..
it marks the day this love was able to form
I felt it soon as i saw the city lights
they say I sound country but I been livin the city life
so i was eager to see what this city like
I been here a millions times before
there are things i've forgot
but imma pick it up like ridin a bike
hopped in the whip spent 2hrs lost but I found what I was lookin for
with each wrong turn I saw a pleasant site
feel rejuvenated full of energy and a restored hunger and thirst
I got a criminal mind but no need to clutch ya purse
today is Sunday so this is my church
my blessin i'm sendin and receivin
my faith ur readin
I'm God's Gift and he told me its my season
I've been humble and loyal neva tempted by treason
now I'm here with this girl
one of the most talked about cities in the world
the place everyone visits
on 285 goin in a circle like a pivot
staring around takin time admirin her beauty
I look at her and see nothin but opportunity
I came to hear, I came to tear
release what's been pinned up
no more jus hangin around like a pin up
here I feel I can prosper

BALANCE

my new love got so much to offer
so much creativity inside
all I need is time
either hers or mine
I've had so many positive and influential convos since I been here
my body just arrived but my heart's been here
got a new call log more people to text
better time to invest
discussin how to future tense the past
we on track and maneuvering the same path
I was born in the city of the GREATEST
since then only a few have really MADE IT
they've all had to leave to do so
I wanna try bein rich cause I've lived my whole life poe
nothin lavish
not interested in millions of dollars on cars and jewelry
ya'll can have it
I just wanna give my moms whatever she need
help my pops reach his dreams
he 63 and be on that shoulda woulda coulda tried but didn't get it
I'm on my do, done, did it, lovin so terrific
ya'll can see it first hand
my blueprint, my thesis to my plan
some of ya'll be confused and tryna figure my purpose.
April 2nd marked my 25th
I'm officially callin this the year of the G.I.F.T.
I ain't gettin no younger
success is the only thing to feed this hunger
my journey started last summer
I'm optimistic on the things I can accomplish
making a promise to me myself and God that imma go hard
fight whatever battle bandage any scar
Happy Birthday Millie!!!
I never forget how when first met u said:
"you're gonna be a star"
and I said:
"it takes one to know one cause you already are"

ya'll takin this journey wit me, when I win we all goin to Disney
IM HERE NOW
where I always wanted to BE
I LOVE ATLANTA
from the feel of it
I THINK SHE LOVE ME

Going to Atlanta was meant to be the fix. It was meant to be the healing. It was meant to be the cleanse. It my opinion, it wasn't meant to go the way it went. It wasn't happening in the manner in which I had expected. Imagine my discouragement, this city was a place I descended upon with the goal to make something out of myself but I struggled there too. The fulfillment I expected never manifested. My pride took a hit. I wanted to be out and about. I wanted to connect but because I felt inadequate, I became reclusive. Thankfully I had Mo, she pushed me. She encouraged me. She believed in me and above all of that she LOVED me. She deserved more than what I could offer. I didn't feel complete with myself. It's hard to even factor other people in your life when you're not happy with your life. She worked a full time job and was going to school. That was a life I knew I couldn't adapt to. It wasn't for me to have a career, so the whole school and work thing never appeased me. We had our disagreements about what she felt like I should do and what I wanted to do. The beauty in our situation was that she needed me just as much as I needed her. For me, I needed love. I needed to build myself back up. During that point of my life I was damaged goods. My trust for people was next to nothing. I had spent the better part of the last two years on a warpath of destruction building myself up then tearing myself down. The consistency I felt with her eased my disdain for the world. The hardest thing to admit is that you're not good enough.

In the city I fell in love with, I found this beautiful girl that fell in love with me but I was going through too much of my own bullsh*t to even realize how amazing she was. How pure she was. How genuine she was. Girls weren't exactly lining up to date college dropouts working part time driving a 1998 Monte Carlo. (I kept it clean tho) It's hard to not look back and cherish that about her. It's not that I want her back, I just wish I would have noticed it then. Thanks to my tutelage,

Mo's a lawyer now which really makes me proud. I was there when she was applying for law school. I admire that she set a goal and did all the things necessary to achieve it. I'm heavy into watching this mini series on FX called "The OJ Vs. People" I joked with her that she's like that female attorney who is Johnnie Cochran's assistant lawyer and we laughed about how she never has any lines. I sent her the first part of the book like a month ago. She read it and liked it. Well, she said it's "readable" which I'm not too sure is a ringing endorsement but she promised not to sue me for mentioning her in the book. If she tries to sue me then this is my proof that she OK'd my mention of her. Be that as it may, that's her way of taking digs at me, she means well. I plan to talk bad about her later on in the book and for good reason but for now, that's still my buddy. It's not always rainbows and butterflies whenever love is involved. We've managed to get to a good place now but we definitely had rough parts.

Speaking of rough parts, 2010 didn't start off good for me to say the least. Maybe my expectations were too high. I expected a change of scenery would instantly fix everything I was going through. When I was writing and posting my poetry on Face and the Book, I didn't have the foresight to know how these things would play into my life. It's cool to document things and be able to go back and follow the timeline of your life. What I wrote foreshadowed why me going to LA was not only necessary but inevitable.

Live & LIVE
January 1, 2010 ·

I feel somethin weighin my heart down
I can see the end but I don't know where to start now
pardon my contrast
I ain't as worst as my last
I wonder if my future is worth my past
cause for now it's my present
not the least bit pleasant
it's not feasible for a peasant
unless you got the work ethic
life don't come easy you just gotta work at it
I've been given somethin let no man take away from it
the night goeth and the day cometh
it's a long climb and a short plumet
I'm cautious in my elevation before I reach my summit
everything I plan to do I've already done it
so i'll be relivin my dreams if I neva wake up
I've known I've slept in peace that won't break up
my outlook is inward
a reflection if you will inverse of the N word
positive from a negative
they tried to kill it
I let it live

I CAN'T GET AWAY SO I CAN NEVER GET A WAY

February 28,2010

Now that that's off my chest
I feel the need to put my dreams to rest
like rims my reality and perceptions are off set
I woke up to realize this monstrous facade
livin is work I've been tempted to quit my job
that's a secret so keep it
I called in sick
puttin a knife 2 my wrist
man I jus need a break like red rear lights to minimize the risk
a precautions warning
a sign a symbol
a note
a message
a tale
a true story
is a lie cause that's somethin you tell
I may prevail
before a wedding head piece
sayin a lot to say the least
I jus wanna say my peace
when can I no longer be concerned
if a fire's never meant to burn
we go from dusk to dawn
to ashes in an urn
a reflection isn't always what you see but what you're shown
born to live just to die alone
I can't find comfort in my home
I fly from it,a Jordan air heiress
spinnin on a Ferris
wheel I learn livin on a terrace
can't give up the chase
when time is runnin like water when its parched
scared scarred only use it when its sparse

I say it as it comes to me
in a room all alone entertaining company
this could never come from me
if I'm feelin comfortably
no comforter can comfort me
better than my mind will
better than these lines feel
I can tell you the truth but be lying still
even if I die i'm never lyin still
Just know I never said it
just like you never read it
out my mind without it being vocal
in the key a of life with no coach to coach you
I can only hope to
if I could i'd hope you
I put it in a note to
place it in harmony like a note do
well all on the same page
it says my name but livin in it the same
sharin my mind is easier than sharin my heart
my love is attached to my fears
my insecurities won't let'em part
I got a visual 9-5
I call it my work of art
I tip toe through the light and run through the dark
take aim with a dart
playin a harp
I cover my pain with a smile
I call it my tarp
I call it my sweet tart
sleepin with a sweetheart
in a mansion livin off street smarts
i'll let it end soon as I know when it starts
Two hands formin a "T"
quick time up 2 draw up the D
nobody keepin score
but for some reason i'm left guardin me

BALANCE

I'm in a zone tryna slow up the game
with no pockets searchin for change
left with nothin forced to live rights
I spend my days in a daze only livin at night
feelin dead wrong yet i'm livin right?
after all livin is life
so they say
I feel I can't get away
I can never get a way.

yall be good. thanks for having me, Gift, you see me.

Location: Los Angeles, CA
Date; April 11, 2010
Time: 1:00AM
Day 7

Uhhh this day 2 of the gym uhh locking up too early and leaving me um with nothing to do last nigh-- yesterday I made it. Today it's 1 o clock they been closed since 8 and I ain't go to sleep last night...I just dosed off like two seconds ago that's why I wanted to take my camera out and bring this up in case I dozed back off and don't wake back up. I'm on a, I'm on a city street as you can see. I put my head, my head on my hand, wait my, my hand on my head, just rested it.. Well I'm about to walk the strip again, that'll give me some energy, see something but yeah I'll check back. One.

Hours later...

Helllo, good morning , let the church say amen, uh Today is April the 11th, 7:43 am and um man I had a night last night not nothing bad but I was soo tired yoo like tired to the point where I was, I was literally sleepwalking. I, I was going in and out of consciousness. It was crazy, one time I just woke up and I was on a bus, I was on a bus stop and like it was a police car to my lef-- right and a fire truck to my left and I was like what happened? But it was funny cause nobody said nothing to me, so I, I don't know why they was even there and so like I just got-- no and so, no I was somebody, I don't know somebody talking to me about "wouldn't you want to say something to your daughter if you had 60 seconds to live? or something so I just got up and walked over to the building and just stood there and security guy just came and did something to the-, I don't, it was weird but yeah that was that. I didn't go to sleep at all. Not even a lick. yeah so um just left Mcdonald's. I was in there chilling, I ain't take a nap in there either. They got

139

*on me last time, they put me out "you've been in here 3
hours sir, you have to go" Well damn, who's counting? You
feel me, but I was in there knocked, I was all over the table,
it was probably embarrassing. I wasn't trying to be discreet
about it either. I was just tired. But yeah today, man, um,
I done, this has been a long week. I've probably slept like
12 hours total and I haven't slept at all like literally the
past two days so especially after what happened last night
when I couldn't I. It was like being high, but I don't do
drugs, I, it was crazy...*

...crazzzy...

Fortunately, reprieve came for me later that day. Thanks to a generous
contribution from LaVon I was able to book a hotel room for the night.
Again, one of the cool things about LA was all the random things I
found myself doing or randomly walking into. On my way to check into
my hotel I had noticed all the streets were blocked off from Sunset to
Hollywood boulevard but didn't know why. As I made my way down
Vine street and turned left on Hollywood boulevard, I noticed a sea
of people walking and chanting. As I got closer I could see that it
was a rally. People were marching and protesting for gay rights and
about getting equal social security benefits for same sex couples. They
marched and chanted:

"What do we want?"

"Benefits!"

"And when do we want them?"

"Now"

They followed that up with:

"Social security! Not insecurities!"

Being that I wasn't sure of the proper marching etiquette, I waited for the crowd to thin out which took a while because there were a lot of people. I seen an elderly guy crossing so I followed his lead. Three blocks and 2 turns later I arrived at the hotel. Finally. Rest!

Location: Los Angeles, CA
Date: April 11, 2010
Time: 9:54am
Day 7

So yeah um, last night I made it to the hotel around 9. I don't remember anything past that because I remember laying down and I woke up around 830. I was mad because I didn't make the full 12 hours but I don't know, it felt good man, I don't even think I turned over the whole night which is, which is great but now watching a little TV. Nothing on really, Sportscenter. Uhh but yeah man look at my feet tho, they're like swollen, you probably can't tell because you never seen them before but they're swollen bad man. I was wondering yesterday because like, I went to buy shoes and all I had are those converses and converses just feels like you walking on the ground too much. You can feel every pebble, every rock, so I'm like I need some new shoes man so I went out to the mall obviously and everything I tried on was tight even the 12s. I was like man why is nothing, nothing fitting me? Then when I got here I took my shoes off and was like dang, that's not the size of my feet. So um, I think I'm um, gonna take it easy today and tomorrow. I was going to do my full out homeless thing but um I don't think that's going to twerk. I can't, I need my feet, I don't want to lose my feet but it's a nice Motel 6. I'm not sure if they left the light on for me but got my um caribbean inspired bed spread. The bed is huge, I didn't take no advantage of it all. I stayed on this side the whole time, didn't roll over or anything...

...Oh they got a fridge in here? Dang, didn't notice that. balling. yeah, nothing, nothing ya know, got the corduroy, what do you call em? Blinds?...

...There go my backpack. It's going on 10, check out is at 11 so gonna go take a shower and let this puppy charge

then um. I don't know what I'm going to do all day. But it's just, it's just weird like, like it's 8 o'clock now, I just woke up. I haven't, you know what I'm saying, I haven't been able to say that in like forever...

...so last night when I got here and I was about to lay down I was just, I hadn't laid down all last week. Like laid down. Like you, You know how you lay in a bed? I haven't laid anywhere. On a couch, on a futon or nothing. Everything I did was sitting in a chair with my head on a table. That was my sleep all last week and it wasn't sleep, it was all naps so like 40 minutes here 40 minutes there 10 minutes here 15 minutes there. That's all I did, like I didn't, there's' no luxury of lying in a bed and just having a cover around you so that just got me like, it made me like, so emotional, like, just so grateful and thankful, like you know what I'm saying, that's the stuff you take for granted, you know what I'm saying? You go home, you kick your shoes, just lay in the bed like oh I'm tired, going to sleep but when you don't do that for so long and you, man, every night, aggggh, I just want to lay down, aagggh, I'm so sleepy. I'm saying this while I'm walking and like the night before last, I don't know if i said this but I'm sure I did but I fell asleep while I was walking. It was just a weird, I don't even know what happened. I fell asleep while I was walking and next thing I knew I woke up and I was on a bench but I don't remember anything in between that and like it was sirens and I was like what happened?...

...And I still don't know what happened. That's crazy to me, so that's how out of it I was. But yeah man I'm blessed, I feel good to be here. I woke up with an enormous amount of flem you call it, snot. So I spent like 5 minutes coughing all that up. I still got some left as you can hear. I'm about to go hop in the shower, get myself together I'mma need about a hour..

...But yeah man me and my slave feet, mass'a don't get me. I'mma show yall, like, hopefully, like nah, they might still be swollen but my feet, my feet are skinny. They ain't this thick, like right here and right here. They're not usually that thick. But I'm in LA watching the news on California. That's crazy. But that's it, singing off, Dipset truly yours. U see me.

Location: Louisville, KY
Date: February 8th, 2016

Welcome back folks!! How are things with you? Anything new or exciting happen since we last talked? I hope so. In my case, I had something very exciting occur. Before leaving the ATL, I was booked again to work on set. Being a huge Tupac fan, It was so awesome to not just be on the set but to actually get to be IN the movie and recreate scenes from his actual life.It was something I would have never dreamed of. They might edit out the scenes I was in but I don't care. Tupac is my all time favorite artist. I grew up listening to his music all the time. Being on the set was cool especially considering how I didn't even know the movie was filming before I got to Atlanta. My life is beyond random. I love that. On any given day there's no telling where I'll be or what I'll be doing.

Writing this book was something I randomly decided to do. This process of writing this book has been so revealing, therapeutic and freeing.It's just like I can feel the process changing me and making me a better person. My initial attempt at self improvement occurred around the age of 22-ish. There was a moment of revelation and realization that I didn't like who I was as a person. I had a bad habit of being manipulative. I've never been a liar but I learned that there was a way to tell the blatant truth but do it in such a blunt and sarcastic manner to make the person not take your reply serious. For example:

Her: *Emmanuel, why didn't you answer your phone or call me back last night?*

Me: *Well, obviously it's because I wasn't home and was over another girl's house. When I saw you call I cut my phone off so you'd think my phone had died. I spent the night there which meant I couldn't call you back because I'd have to explain to her why I'm on the phone talking to another girl so I just didn't bother calling you back. Duh.*

Her: *uughhh you play too much, why can't you ever tell the truth?*

Me: *I just did.*

Her: *Nevermind*

My maturation started to matriculate towards my quest to be a better person. From then on out I started to work towards this ultimate "destiny" I've grown into. I didn't know what exactly it was I was working toward, I just knew I had to change my life. Ten years later, it all makes sense. Everyday it makes more and more sense why I'm here. Everyday I'm striving to fulfill my destiny.

That's crazy but that's it singing off Dipset truly yours. U see me.

Location: Los Angeles, CA
Date: April 12, 2010
Time: 12:11am PST
Day 8

After a much needed and well deserved night of rest. I exited the hotel refreshed and reinvigorated, poised to finish this journey. The first thing I did was visit this homeless shelter I had looked up a few days prior on 6636 Selma St. After a few minutes of being lost, I finally made it to the shelter where I encountered an elderly woman standing in front. She was a short adorable woman. Her chin length grey hair was covered with a winter cap. She was standing there with a couple of plastic bags on each side of her on the ground as she adjusted her full length brown jacket. While I was looking around she got my attention...

Woman

Can you give me some money? I'm homeless...

Gift

Is this the homeless shelter?

Woman

What?

Gift

Is this the homeless shelter?

Woman

No, this is the place that gives you clothes, you can take a shower. where are you from?

Gift

Kentucky

Woman

Could you give me some money a couple of dollars. a 5 or 10?

Gift

(laughing playfully) A 5 or 10? You went from change to a dollars now you want 10 dollars?

Woman

Well, What you can afford.

Gift hands her a dollar.

Gift

There you go. That's a hundred dollars right there.

Woman

Beautiful, where can I get a hundred for it?

Gift

That's a one hundred dollar bill right there in your hand.

Woman

How do I get a hundred?

Gift

(smiling) Look, it says 100, it's Kentucky money.

Woman

Aw you're drugged up?

Gift

(laughing) Na, Not yet. So you you just sign in or just go in there?

Woman

I think they're closing but you can check.

Gift

I'm just doing some research, for a school project.

Woman

What school?

Gift

Uh, University of Gift.

Woman

Of who?

Gift

Gift.

Woman

G-I-F-T?

Gift

Yes ma'am!

Woman

I'm a gift...

Gift

Everybody is.

Woman

...Gift of god.

Gift

Amen!

Woman

Black and white.

Gift

Right, do you know the hours it's open or anything?

Woman

It opens at 7:30 in the morning.

Gift

And then closes around this time?

Woman

I think so.

Gift

Well, you have a good one.

Woman

Thanks for the dollar.

Gift

(laughing) It's a hundred dollars.

Woman

How can I get a hundred for it?

Gift

Just tell them Gift gave it to you, they'll help you out.

There's a normality that manifests itself after you've went through something. You get accustomed to going without. You get accustomed to not having. After that first week in LA, I began to adapt and grow accustom to the change. I began to grow accustom to the adversity in front of me. In time, I had developed a routine. I had FINALLY got rest and started to turn that corner of being lost and heading towards adjusting. The worst of the worst was over. The fact that I made it through it all gave me hope to push forward. Once you go long enough without having or doing something, you forget that you used to have it. Something is to be said about that convo with the elderly woman outside of the homeless shelter. It reminded me of the lady who was telling me about the rosebud and how she kind of shared this prophecy about my life with me. The whole entire premise of going to LA was spiritually based and as I think back, I think those two individual ladies were angels in some capacity. They both referenced God and had a symbolic disposition. They always say "...you find God in the most unpredictable and unforeseen places..." That's what brings me comfort. Things happening organically and naturally and by chance mean the most to me.

Chance has been a common thread in my life. Well, what others call chance. I consider it being the higher power I believe in putting me where I should be at all time. In short, I consider it my destiny. For example, after leaving the homeless shelter, I walked around the town and came across a nice red grocery store shopping cart. I decided to take it. I pushed that cart down Hollywood Blvd proudly. The fact that people didn't stare or wonder what I was doing was odd. I expected people to look at me and give me a face like *"what is he doing?"* Seeing somebody pushing a shopping cart down the street was far more common than I thought. If I were to push a shopping cart down the street in Louisville I could be sure that I'd get stares from people. Not in LA. I pushed my cart all the way to the library and parked it outside, turning it upside down so that it discouraged anybody from coming by and trying to take it. After spending two hours in the library, I pushed the cart over to my gym on Sunset blvd. As I mentioned before, My gym was attached to ArcLight Cinema. Unbeknownst to me, the "Death at a Funeral" premiere was going on. I ditched my cart after I noticed people forming around this guardrail close to the red carpet. I walked over to join them. It either rained or was expected to rain because the red carpet was covered by this plastic tent. Not sure if any of you remember of saw the movie but it starred Chris Stone, Marvin Lawrence, Tracy Freeman and had a gang of other well known actors in it. I went from pushing a grocery cart to being 15 feet from people I had always watched and seen on TV. "Marvin" was my third favorite show growing up. That show and the movie "Boys Bad" was a couple of the reasons that I wanted to be on TV and be in movies. To be able to see him in person, especially given the pretense of why I was in LA had a deeper meaning to me.

Many times in life, we think we want something until we get it and see it's not all that it's cracked up to be. I learned that lesson quickly when I got back from LA. Shortly after I got back to Atlanta, I met J through a mutual associate. J is a publicist and major power player in the city. Working with her was what I guess you could call my "big break" She gave me the platform to chase my dreams and see them firsthand. The closer I got, the more and more I realized my vision getting blurry. The first event I worked was her company's Anniversary party that was held at the former mansion of Hollywood heavyweight Pyler Terry. It was now owned by his business partner at the time who just so happened to be one of her clients. For me, the crazy take away from the party was that from the people who I met nobody knew I was a nobody. As J introduced me to everybody I never felt overwhelmed or out of my element. Here I was, a poor kid from Louisville, shaking hands and having small talk with people I grew up watching on TV and in films. The same people I heard on radio interviews and read articles about took an interest in things I had to say. I was just the dude keeping the bar stocked with ice, helping with Valet and anything else I had to do like coordinate people doing their interviews in the home theatre. I wasn't in a nice fancy tux, I had on a t-shirt and bball shorts but as one girl I met there later told me, her and the girls she was sitting with took notice of me and thought I was somebody important because I was speaking to everybody and was all over the house like I knew where everything was. I did. I had been there hours before the first person showed up helping to decorate. The perception was that I must be somebody if I'm at this event. I wasn't. Well, at least I thought I wasn't. With each event I felt more and more liked I belonged.

The thing with belonging is that you become privy to information the general public isn't aware of. Being a public figure is highly stressful and strenuous. What I learned is that that smile for the camera might be the only time these people have smiled that entire day. There are several dark moments. Several instances when you're forced to compromise, forced to say and do things you really don't want to do in order to appease others and to stay in the public eye. This was always my dream and what I wanted. I would have done anything to be around these people in my younger years. Would have gave anything to be at these movie premieres and go to these parties. Once I got to those places I learned that it isn't the dream I wanted at all. It was extremely humbling. It was eye opening. It was destiny. My destiny linked me with the right person and I walked right behind the velvet rope. Didn't have to kiss ass, didn't have to sell my soul to get there. I'm grateful for that, grateful for the experiences. It helped me stay on path and not veer from this journey I'm on now.

What they never tell you, or what you never see is how hard it is to be successful. How much of a struggle it is to trust those around you. When you're talking to people, who from your own perception are on top of the world and have all the things you can only dream of, you realize that the thing that you have is something they aren't privileged to have. Honesty. Truth. When you're successful, everybody around you becomes people who will do or say just about anything to appease you. Some will get close just to use you. The thing that kept me away from falling into that category was the fact that I knew I didn't want people around me who weren't genuine. The energy I give off is sincere and genuine. The successful people I met gravitated to that energy and confided with me exactly what Biggie said "More money. More problems." There's an immense pressure to maintain that level of success. While maintaining it you lose sight of what it's like to be yourself. What it's like to be in touch with reality. There's so many built up facades that people have to hide who they are in order to keep that level of success. Being around that and witnessing how miserable some of these people were really detracted me from wanting money, fame and anything that came with it.

Society defines "success" by sums and status. That's not the success I want. I want to help others more than I help myself. That's success to me. I want to be successful in influencing people to live their dreams. Successful in helping those who are unfortunate and for whatever reason are down on their luck to have outlets and resources to better their lives.

There's a movie called "The Joneses" that's really insightful to the idea and concept of perceptions and these ideals of what success is. The movie really makes you think. It plays off the saying "Keeping up with the Jones's". *SPOILER ALERT* In the movie, the neighbor of the Jones's ends up killing himself. He became so desperate to live the life that his neighbors lived. So much so that he maxed out his credit cards and didn't make mortgage payments just so he could buy lavish things. He became fixated on how seemingly perfect the life of his neighbors was. He fell for the perception of perfection. To him, they were successful and lived an amazing life. In all actuality, the Jones's were paid to market and promote this perfect lifestyle. They were hired and funded by a corporation to move into the neighborhood and influence their neighbors to buy these products such as cars, clothes etc. They held parties at their house just to show off all the things they had. They were basically like a living commercial and using product placement to create these perfect perceptions. Their neighbor was oblivious of that facade and literally killed himself trying to live like them. Ironic right?

In all honesty, on a day to day basis, I don't care if I live or die. Each day to me feels like bonus time. It's like when you feed the meter. This is all just extra time for me. I should of died two tries ago so I refuse to live my life for appeasement and approval of others. I'm not willing to die to live the life others feel I should live. I'm not willing to create a facade just to fit it. I'm confident enough in my destiny to shoulder all the ridicule that's placed on me for living the lifestyle I live. What people don't realize is that this is a facade free life. I'm not out putting up a good public image. I don't care if people know I'm broke or not because guess what, I'm broke! Most people will hide that and do dumb things so that they don't appear to be poor or to make sure people know they aren't poor. There are people who I know who own cars they can't afford and are barely able to pay their car note and rent. There are people I've known who had a nice house and nice things that they obtained doing fraudulent things. There are people doing years in prison because they were involved in criminal activity all for the purpose of obtaining things they felt they need or wanted just to fit in into society.

Ask me what I consider society.

A facade.

This society had me doubting my life

This society had me questioning my existence

This society made me believe that I wasn't good enough

This society has tainted views on love

This society has tainted views on morals, values and religion

This society helped me to realize I'm different

This society helped me obtain my identity

This society helped me see what not to do

This society is your perception

This society is yours

This society is you.

VIII

My Angel

Once upon a time, not long ago, there was a beautiful soul that became a fixture in my life who, for all intent and purposes, I'll just refer to as "My Angel".

We met 10-ish years ago on the palatial campus of Western Kentucky University. I don't remember the first time I saw her but I do remember the first time I remember seeing her for the first time. Let me set the scene. It was a lovely autumn-ish day in October-ish. I was wearing... I don't remember. Come to think of it, I don't remember much about that day. It may not have even been October. Aside from that, I remember everything about that day. I was sitting in my Spanish 101 class talking with TT, (who just had a beautiful baby girl a few months ago! CONGRATULATIONS TT!!!!) and in walks, yep, you guessed it. A girl with whom I had had past history with. "*Oh crap!*". As I'm processing how to diffuse a potential disaster, things went from bad to worst for me. Members of the WKU women's basketball team walk in. Guess who walks in with them. Yep, you guessed it. My Angel!!!!! Soon as I saw her I did a triple double, triple quadruple take. It was almost physically impossible to turn my head away from her without looking right back at her. My eyes just wouldn't stop looking at her and for good reason. I'm not going to describe how beautiful she is and talk about how her long dark curly haired flowed like an appalachian waterfall down her back. Nor will I make mention of how her almond brown skin glistened like the sun reflecting off a pond in the hills of Argentina. Nope. I'll just let you try to paint a picture of her in your own manner. As I gawked at her, time froze. Nothing around me seemed to exist. It almost felt like everything was moving in slow motion and a person with a harp was sitting on a cloud playing the intro to "Back that thing up" by Geriatric. That was until TT slapped my leg to get my attention. As I wiped the drool from my mouth with the sleeve of my shirt I turned to TT to see what she wanted. Then turned my eyes back to My Angel and admired her for a tad bit more.

Everything I did in that class from that point on was done strategically just to get her attention. I'd stand up and stretch for no reason. She sat in the first row by the door so I walked in late to class on purpose so she'd have to see me walk in. Whenever the teacher asked for a volunteer or for somebody to answer a question I raised my hand at speeds that would put the speed of light and sound to shame. Spanish came easy to me, I always knew the answer and hoped that'd she'd be smittened by my bilingualness. These sad attempts were the best I could do. For that whole semester I don't think I spoke two words to her directly. Me and TT were like an unofficial couple so I couldn't really maneuver around that enough to be able to frolic around with My Angel in class or outside of class for that matter.

Fast forward with me to a few months later. As fate would have it, me and my angel befriended each other! We had mutual friends so our paths crossed. One mutual friend in particular proved to be detrimental to my hopes of having a storybook romance with My Angel. Look, I'll just go ahead and say it, The ladies love me. As a young man in college, I didn't shy away from that. My reputation among the women's basketball team was there before My Angel joined the team. Her first introduction of me happened long before she walked into that Spanish class. I was "property" of somebody else on her team. Prior to her I had had another situationship with another girl on the team. For that reason, My Angel never really looked at me in that manner even tho as I would find out later, she had a HUGE CRUSH ON ME!!!! Guess how I found out, the girl on the basketball team of whose "property" I was told me. My Angel had mentioned me to her but told her that since she had claimed me should wouldn't bother. With my newfound knowledge I asked My Angel about it and she confirmed it. Unfortunately, by this time she was in a relationship so it wasn't anything either of us could act on so we became platonic friends. I valued and cherished our bond. She was so shy and soft spoken but had such an amazing heart and genuine demeanor. She was very studious, mature and responsible. All the things I wasn't. That made me admire her more. She didn't enjoy going out or partying. She'd rather study or practice basketball. I fell in love with her heart. I fell in love with her morals. I fell in love with her integrity. I fell in love with her humility I fell in love with her smile. I fell in love with..... her!

Over the next few years we kept in touch via Face and the Book from time to time sending messages to each other sharing details about our lives. The weird dynamic of our friendship was that we'd talk about her relationships and I'd encourage her to work things out with the guy she was with. I wanted to see her happy. Even if it wasn't with me. She deserved that. This would seem like the perfect time for me to capitalize on her relationship woes and interject how I could love her better but I didn't. I just knew that if it was meant to be then it would be. There was one time in particular when her and her boyfriend broke up officially and she sent me a message. It was a very in depth and detailed conversation. This was when she conceded that she had more than just a crush on me. She told me that she noticed me as soon as she walked into Spanish class. She told me of how she took notice of how intellectually gifted I was. That made her crush on me even harder. This was my first time hearing this and it excited me. YES!!!!! MY CRUSH LIKES ME!!!! She told me of how once she hugged me for the first time. She told me she felt so close and comfortable to me. She told me that she wished I hadn't let go. I told her I felt the same way then we pondered, Where do we go from here? The answer to that question would just have to wait. Eventually she ended up getting back with her ex. Cue the violin. Cue the sad face emoji. Cue the crying Jordan meme.

More time passed. More seasons changed before we spoke again The next time we had talked was in told me that she had broke up with her ex. YAY!!!! Then she told me that she had a new boyfriend. NOO!!!! At any rate, I was happy to hear that she was doing well. She had graduated with a degree in Biology and now was working on her Master's. Anybody want to take a stab at which state she was living in? Yep. you guessed it.

Fiver years of anxiety had me fidgeting like a 6 yr old trying to hold their urine while waiting in line at a public restroom. At any moment she'd be pulling up. There was so much excitement. Finally I'd get to see something familiar. I'd finally get to hear a voice I heard. I'd finally get to do something other than wander the streets of Hollywood for hours. My phone rung: "*Hey, Where are you? I'm driving down Sunset blvd right now...*" The sound of her voice instantly brightened up my day. The site of her face took my soul to another hemisphere. There she was. It was deja vu all over again. I couldn't take my eyes off her. As she drove she talked to me while pointing out landmarks and telling me about the city. She took me around the neighborhood she grew up and shared with me what it was like growing up there. She was intent on making sure I had the full Los Angeles experience. She took me to all the happening places and the must eat places like Repo's Waffles and Chicken, Burger Fat, Out & In and blessed me with what came to be my greatest joy. TACO TUESDAYS!!!!! Being with her made me feel human again.I was relieved. I finally had a moment of comfort. I finally had a moment of certainty. I finally had a moment of security.

There aren't any words to put into context my level of desperation while living on the street. It was such a lonely experience. It was so hard to adjust. Hard to adapt. I found myself in a dark place. Her being there was a Godsend. Just imagine being in a place 25000 miles from where you grew up. 25000 miles from anything you can readily identify. 25000 miles from a face you recognize. 25000 miles from any sounds that sound familiar. Imagine that. It was unlike normal life. I realized that nobody gives a sh*t about you, nobody says hi to you. Nobody bothered to ask me how my day was. As I suffered, the world continued to exist around me. Nobody cared how hungry I was. Nobody cared how sleepy I was. Nobody cared about me. It made stop caring about myself. It's so easy to lose touch with reality in that environment. As I felt my grip slipping, My Angel brought me back. There were times when reality felt so distant. Many times, I lost perspective. Many times, I struggled. Around her my desperation didn't show. That's because it didn't exist. In those times, I found hope. That night she laid that blanket over me after I fell fast asleep on the couch, was symbolic of that hope. I felt covered. I felt safe as soon as I looked into her eyes.

When I decided to take my journey and leap of faith to LA, I talked to her and told her. She of course thought what I was planning to do was insane but she insisted that I call her when I got out to LA so we could catch up and do lunch. She provided me with much more than lunch.

She provided me with comfort. She provided me with peace of mind. She provided me with love. If I was to take the time I spent with her out of the equation, then I don't honestly know how I would have managed. Before I left Atlanta, It wasn't apparent to me how much I'd need her because I seriously had no intentions of seeing her often. I wanted to really divulge into this role of being deprived by submerging myself into the pain, anguish and fear that was sure to come. What I learned was that I wasn't prepared to be prepared. Life is humbling. That experience was severely overwhelming. I'm eternally grateful to God for placing Her Angel there to help me make it through it. Adversity isn't an easy hill to climb. It will break you down. It will throw you for loops. It will put you in situations you never would have imagined. Adversity will make you question your place in life. Adversity will make you question your purpose in life. Before I was forced to answer those questions My Angel showed up.

I'll never be able to thank you enough for how much you were there for me. That whole experience was physically and mentally draining but through it all I found strength in knowing I had you there. It's so somber and sad to even write about right now. I'm grateful for you. I'm getting teary eyed right now because life doesn't give us too many genuine people like you. I was fortunate enough to have you when I needed you the most. You're the first person in my life that I knew LOVED me. Not only did you love me but you loved me for me. You were there when I literally had nothing. There when I was wearing the same clothes for days. There when I was losing my sanity. There when my life was changing, There when I was getting ridiculed for doing it. There when I was realizing how flawed the world was. There when I had lost hope. There when I wanted to give up. There when I cried. There when I wanted to die. There when I didn't have money to feed myself. There when I felt the world crashing down around me. Through it all, you never judged me. You were there to tell me you were proud of me. You were there to give me strength. You were there to tell me I'm doing something amazing. You were there to hug me. You were there to hold me. You were there to tell me you were there for me. You never ridiculed me, you were compassionate enough to understand what I was doing and show your admiration of me for it. I love that you never questioned or doubted me. I love that you never tried to get me to stop. I love that you related to what I was doing even though it was a far departure from your life. I love that you took time from your day to check on me. I love that you thought enough of me to take me places and show me things I would have never noticed or seen while I was there. I love that I love...... You!

I miss you with all my heart and love you with even more of it.

Location: Washington, DC
Date: March 23, 2016
Time: 1:11pm EST

Morning Folks! Just for clarity, I wrote that chapter about "My Angel" months ago but since I had extended my content for the book, it kept getting pushed down. The place where it is now, falls into place of when I first met up with her while I was there which was on April 14, 2010. Since my last entry in February, I've been doing a lot of editing of the things I already wrote up to this point and also going back to watch the footage. It gets very tamed. The bulk of the days are far less eventful. There's nothing worth taking time to transcribe out of those 26 days except for two more days. I'll get around to that eventually.

(**Editing notes** December 12, 2016. I just got choked up editing that last page. I still love you Bria!)

March 14th was my mom's birthday. HAPPY BIRTHDAY MOMA!!!!!!! LOVE YOU!!!!!!!! Ask me how I spent it. Icing and elevating my ankle. Ready for some irony? It's the very same ankle that I injured that kicked off my whole life awakening way back in 2008-ish. I hadn't got hurt since. When it happened I was in at the gym in Louisville Fitness doing what I do best:

Get Buckets!

Slow motion reading taking place in 5,4,3,2..... I was driving to the rim, in dominant fashion, poised to make yet another spectacular play. I dribbled from left to right, right to left. Between one leg. Between the other leg. Then in a flash, I blew past the sucka attempting to guard me with a hesitation crossover move. It was in that moment that I got fouled by a helpless jive turkey who had came over to offer help defense. The force pushed me off balance, then... Snap, Crackle,POP! How many of you have ever played with bubble wrap? That's exactly what it sounded like when I rolled my ankle. Fortunately, this time, I was able to still walk, albeit gingerly. Unlike the last time, I didn't collapse to the ground and talk to God. This time I remained upright and walked very sophisticatedly directly to retrieve my personal belongings and the basketball I had checked out, returned it to the front desk then went right to the locker room. And, scene. The swelling in my ankle has went down but the pain is still persistent and annoying. I just want to literally rip my ankle off right now. It sucks being limited. When I was in Louisville those two days after I got hurt, I had to crawl up the steps. That took me back to that feeling of being alone in my apartment. Take it from me, That's not feeling you want to harken back to.

Many people urged me to go to the doctor this time because of how hard it was for me to walk and how much pain I was in. For me, I knew it wasn't anything severe and that there wasn't any structural damage. It was just swollen badly. I soaked and iced it all last week. This week it's been feeling a lot better. I've been able to walk and put more weight on it. That was until I decided to jog from the driveway to across the street and back. BIG MISTAKE. My ankle wasn't ready for that much force and physical exertion. That has led to me being back at square one.e. It's sooo frustrating. I loathe being idle. I lack patience. I loathe that feeling of not being able to do what I want to do. I loathe being physically limited. I figured that since I can't walk, I midas well write and do some editing. So, here I am.

Location: Washington DC
Date: March 25th, 2016
Time: 11:37 am EST

HAPPY BIRTHDAY CALEB!!!!!!!!!!!!!!!!!!!

Lydia gave birth around 3am this morning back home in Louisville. I woke up to a pic of my new nephew. It's sooo fascinating to know what he looks like now. It's soo weird to me that he was in my sister's stomach two weeks ago. Now he's like a person and stuff. He has eyes, hands, ears, feet, arms, and a dimple on his left cheek, just like me. Clearly I have o experience with having or making a baby but I texted my sister this morning she said *"His delivery was the best"*.

Not to say creating life is similar in full totality to my experience of writing this book but I think you can draw some comparisons between the two. This process has taken well around like 9 months in total. Last June, I wrote the initial Prologue for the book. In October, I started working on the book continuously once I got to LA. It's fascinating to see it all come together. When it's finally done it'll be like having a baby. It's something that I've produced. Something I've spent months planning and preparing for. A labor of love if you will. The people who know I'm writing the book have expressed excitement and anticipation of me finishing the book much like waiting for the arrival of a baby. I doubt I'll have a book shower but wrap your minds around this; Book and baby both are four letter words that start with the letter "B" so there's that. Coincidence? I think not. As I write this, I have o indications, inclinations for how this book will end. I still haven't finished talking about what happened in LA or how when I got back from LA I relapsed and fell into dealing with another bout of depression and loss my will to live. Then there's my military experience of joining the Air Force in 2013-ish.

My end goal is just to inspire people to persevere and to never give on yourself. There has been a lot of learning experiences and valuable lessons I've been fortunate to experience in my life and if I can share those lessons and somehow inspire and motivate others then I'd be immensely pleased.

I just want to take this time to express gratitude to EVERYBODY that has helped me along the way. My 8th English teacher at Kammerer Middle School, Mrs. Gleason allowed me start a countdown to my birthday on the chalkboard. Everyday I updated the number of days left until my birthday and everyday she left it up there. She had a conversation with me once and expressed how she admired my sarcasm, wit and intelligence. She told me she felt like I had the potential to be something. I've never forgot that. It still inspires and motivates me to know that you saw that in me at 12 years old. Thank you for that Mrs. Gleason. God Bless You.

Location: Washington, DC
Date: April 2, 2016
Time: 2:46 PM EST

IT'S MY BIRTHDAY SNITCHES!!!!!!!

This has by FAR been the most subdued birthday I've ever had. Not to say I don't care about my birthday but I care less than I've ever cared. It's kind of like how I view all other holidays. Why put so much emphasis into one singular day and make that day special when everyday is and should be treated special? It all feels so disingenuous and forced to get text or face and the book post from people I never talk to. It's a kind gesture but I'm over all that. It's MY day so I spend it as I wish and it doesn't involve a bounty of doing stuff to celebrate it. I just want to stay low key. I woke up, gave thanks and props to the spirit in the sky that I believe in for the ability to see another day, then kept it pushing.

The special thing for me is that I FINALLY got to start back running this week. My ankle is still sore but when you step on the scale and it says 227 three weeks after you saw 202 on it, you spring into action. I've been running everyday this week, I started just doing 2.5 miles then did 5, 4 and 4.02 miles respectfully. I feel alot better and healthy. I still have a way to go before I really feel good and for my ankle to heal. My vertical movements as far as jumping are still restricted. I could probably jump over a phone book but that's it. To "celebrate' my birthday I've been going through and converting video files to watch and help me finish telling the story of my journey. I got a bit emotional and excited upon realizing that I'm almost to the END!!

Since my last LA update, when I spent time with my Angel, I spent those next few days literally not doing anything. My ankle and lower part of my leg swelled up pretty bad. There weren't many options for me so I just tried to rest and do as little walking as possible. I established a routine of icing then soaking my ankle in the hot tub at the gym. In the midst of this, I did make time to go back and revisit the center where I met the elderly woman. This time I went inside. It had various rooms where people could get clothes from. There were bathrooms for people to take showers in. They had a kitchen where people could grab breakfast. There was also a patio area that people utilized to smoke cigarettes and talk amongst themselves. Those conversations were epic. They were surprising very normal. They reminded me of any conversations you'd hear in a barber shop or any place where middle aged men debated about sports, music, the goverment, and women.

The next thing I wanted to experience for myself was what it's like to panhandle. That didn't last long but I gave it a valiant effort. Are any of you familiar of a song by Faka Wlocka entitled "Oh let's do it"? If you are then you'll understand why my panhandling sign that I made using a brown paper grocery bag said "I F*cked my money up, now I can't re-up. Homeless. Please help ;)" After making the sign, I kind of loss the desire to sit or stand and hold a sign so I had the idea to wear the sign. I folded it into the waistband of my shorts so that only the "Homeless. Please Help :)" portion of the sign showed. With my sign on full display I walked down Yucca st right around the corner from the Capitol Records building. I made it like a block and a half before I came across a lady who saw the sign and read it. I asked her if she had any change she'd like to give, she reached in her purse and gave me a dollar. It was surprising as to how quickly I was able to get money. After walking a little further, guilt settled in. I felt fraudulent. Sure I was homeless living on the streets and really needed money but it felt dishonest. It felt like I was stealing and taking from those who really, really, really, really, really, really, really, really, really, really needed it. It almost felt like I was making a mockery of people's real life circumstances and that's something I never wanted to do. That's why I never engaged or interacted with any homeless people. I didn't want to feel like a pariah who was only interested in knowing their story for my own personal gain simply to exploit their story for the purpose of making a documentary. I ended up giving that dollar the lady gave me to another homeless person. As they say, you can't really imagine something until you put yourself in other people's shoes. Being given a dollar made me feel like charity and made me feel like I was stealing but under other circumstances that dollar would of been well received. There were other times during my trip when I was really, really hungry and would of made the most of that dollar. When she gave it to me I really didn't need it. Much like everything else during that trip, I adapted. I made things work in my favor, I found a way. Things began to feel normal to me. It got to a point when things weren't actually that bad.The fear of the unknown was gone. I new what to expect each day so that gave me some sort of comfort.

My friend gave me the idea of spending a night in a "Hostel" My first thought was, *"HECK NO!"* I had saw that movie called "Hostel" and I'll never go out like that Jack!. Obviously, I never knew it was a real thing here. She told me about one in Hollywood. It's only like $28 bucks a night! For a guy who had been reduced to not sleeping, it was worth checking out. My Hostel experience was pleasant. The room was 16x14 with 3 bunk beds in it. Down the hall there were bathrooms and showers. It wasn't a hole in the wall, it was clean and well kept. I was comfortable there. That comfort faded fast.

Location; Los Angeles, CA
Date: April 18, 2010
Day 14

Singing

> These are my confessions...

Speaking

> But yeah um just got off the phone with a lady friend
> of mine and it's nothing really, nothing to share but
> just an overall situation to share but what movie is of
> any good without a love story of some kind, so this is
> my love story man?

> Um I'm single, I've been single. I love being single and
> it's not really something I'm willing to change. I'm willing
> to change until that change is compromised and the
> conversation I just had really compromised my change.
> Umm I was kind of ummm, ummm, open minded if you
> will to changing, accepting to changing but it's that trigger
> of doubt and mistrust that comes apart when you're
> dealing with somebody on that level. So It's hard for me
> to trust people. It's hard for me to open up to people, but
> once I do, then the more, more critical, the more hard on
> you that I am and it's just not for everybody man.
> Love is universal, love is all these great things but for all
> the beauty that it is, it's ugly. I ain't in love but it was cool
> while it was cool. But you know how you just know when
> something's over? like even before you even acknowledged
> that it's over, you just got that feeling like it's about to be
> over or near the end? I just got that feeling man.
> I don't require much, I'm a simple dude. You see
> where I'm at, I'm in a room with 6 bunk beds. I'm low
> maintenance, all I ask is honesty man. Honest and trust.
> I be honest with you and you be honest with me. It's

unfortunate that I'm so smart and intelligent that nothing gets past me. Like I remember stuff that most people won't remember. Like I was talking about this earlier, like the hardest thing to remember is a lie that you make up on the fly. So If I hit you with one question, bam, I don't do follow questions. I hit you with one question "Where were you at?" "uhh such and such and such" alright bam. That's your answer, that's your lie on the fly and I'm going to remember that, then your character, how you act, I''m going to remember all of that stuff. Mannerisms, I notice everything about people, so once you start changing, I'm going to notice that you don't act the same. There's a reason for change. Everybody changes for a reason. So the reason you're not acting the same towards me means you might be sharing that time acting that way towards somebody else.

That's when the light bulb in my head clicks that I gotta put that guard back up. I let it down briefly, If you don't get over, don't get over it then ay, there's nothing I can do for you. I've been single 6 years shawty, that ain't something you're going to give up overnight.

It is what it is man. I love love. I love people, I love to be a around people but I'm not willing to give up, give it up. Can't give up my heart for something that ain't 100%. If it ain't 100% then we can't deal. But I respect that said person still, still got love for them, still going to be cool. Since I've been gone, it's kind of been on the down but that conversation was the icing on the cake. It wasn't even bad. We wasn't going at each other. The person probably don't know how I feel right now because I was just having general conversation but within that general conversation I was analyzing and rationalizing the moods and motives of that person. I just realized it ain't for me man. If you got somebody you love, then love them. If not, then leave them. It's quite simple, don't force nothing.

Location: Los Angeles, CA
Date: April 21, 2010
Time: 5:52am PST
Day 17

Um what it is folk, It's um April 21st, 5:52 am. Chilling at Mcdonalds, just got done eating my sausage biscuit. Didn't go to sleep last night obviously, but uh, I had a good day yesterday. I was in the gym basically all day killing cats. Just doing what I do but I also had another interesting day because a few people brought to my attention that um they don't understand, the whole, my whole thing about what I'm doing or trying to do. Apparently the term homeless is taken to the most literal extent as it can be. As I was explaining to them, I can't be homeless. It's impossible for me to be homeless because so many people care about my well being. So it's like, um, I had every intention of being homeless but like, um, people look out for me. Yet and still, I'm 3000 miles, if not more away from where I'm from. I've never been in Cali, I came, I didn't know what to expect when I came here. I just came here with a backpack, that's it. I didn't, I wasn't banking on anyone doing this or doing that for me, but it just turned out that people have. Even that alone, you can't frown on that. That takes heart, that takes guts I don't know too many who would do that. I came here to go all out but it just ain't end up that way because people care about me. I'm loved. But the experience in itself is still 100.

I did it.

Nobody else was doing it.

So no, I'm not, I can't be homeless, I'm not sleeping on the streets but in the same since, I'm not sleeping in a hotel. I'm not sleeping at all matter fact. I came April 5th, today is the 21st, in that time frame I've slept like through the night slept, 4 times, 4 times that's it. And I'm talking about actually laying down sleeping. Like I get naps every once in awhile but that's 4 times in that time frame. That in itself is a sacrifice, it's all a sacrifice. I'm not out here having fun, I'm not living a lavish life up in the W every night or riding around in a Lambo. But I'm not struggling as bad as people want me to struggle or maybe I'm not, I'm not, I don't have the right attitude about it. I can't help that I'm a positive person, I can't help that I can adapt so easily and be in my own comfort zone. I mean, I guess it would feel better if I was complaining all the time. If I was so depressed, if I was saying how much I hated it. but I mean until you do it, you can't really speak for me. Like I'm doing it, I did it. I've been through, It's not easy, it's not a cakewalk but the thing is I'm good man. I handled it. 4 days of sleep since April 5th. Today's the 21st, and you only got 4 days of sleep every other day you're walking around, ankles swelled up on you, couldn't walk for like a week. Come on now, that ain't fun, that ain't a vacation. People think I'm having a vacation like living it up. I eat Mcdonalds everyday. I'm on a budget. The first 3 days was as legit as it could get. I was crying. I cried. That ain't everyday stuff, but for what it is man, I did something in my heart that um, I was told to do. I believe in what I'm doing. I believe that it's all got a purpose but everything ain't for everybody. So for those having a hard time grasping what's going on then wait for the next bus.

Until you know me, you can never know me.

Location: Los Angeles, CA
Date: April, 22, 2016
Time: 12:46pm PST

Insert a looong deep yaaaaawwwnnn

Salutations world, as you can see, I'm back in LA. Let's do a quick recap. Since my last entry on April 2nd, I left DC, drove to NYC with lovely then drove back to DC. That next day I caught the bus back to NYC and flew back to LA on April 13th. Quick hello and hey to Thi Thi aka my soulmate. She's one of the coolest people I know. Thank you for being a friend.

Soooooo, since I've been back in LA, I did some background acting, well, audience work here and there. Aside from that, I've been mentally preparing and prepping for finishing this here book!!!!! Good news, I've been able to go running and play basketball which I haven't been able to do for a month. The crazy thing is that some gains come with additional losses. It's almost like it's impossible for everything in your life to be going right in your life simultaneously. That being said. Unfortunate news, I couldn't find the other SD card where I had footage of my time in LA.-crying face emojii- I thought it was in KY along with my camera in my backpack. I had my brother looking for it. He told me it wasn't in there. Always the resourceful type, I tried to find ways around not having the SD card by using my social media post from those days to put a timeline of events together but there were still gaps. Always the resourceful type, I decided to essentially relive the experience and go back to living on the street and keep a journal for the last few days. Since the last footage I had was from April 21st, 2010. My goal was to go from April 21st- May 5th living on the street and seeing what transpires.

When I left LA for Dallas on Christmas Eve, I left my Air Force backpack at my friend's place and took another backpack. (waddup Bevy and thank you for everything!!!) Today, I was going through my military backpack putting stuff I didn't need in the bag and guess what I find! My camera along with the SD card!!! I totally forgot I had left it in there. Yaayy!!!!! My joy was short lived because the SD card was somehow corrupted. It wouldn't give me access to the files. Nooo!!! The only way to watch the footage was on the camera itself but I don't have the charger for it. To make matters worse, my laptop battery is officially at its end. My laptop only works when it's plugged into the charger. As you can tell, there's a lot of moving parts that go into writing your first book about things you vaguely remember and need references to actually depict the sequence of events properly.

Editing Notes The SD card I found turned out to not be the SD card with the rest of the footage from my 26 days on it. That SD card is officially lost.

That's why I'm so tired right now. I had the bright idea that if I were going to recreate those days from when I lived on the streets then I'd need to deprive myself of sleep so that I had that same feeling I did when I went through it initially. In preparation of that I've been sleeping as little as possible lately .I've slept like maybe 20 hours since I got here last Wednesday and that's because my body is still on East Coast time. I've been waking up at 6am PST everyday. These days pales in comparison to what I actually did previously. Sleep deprivation was the biggest hurdle I had to overcome. That feeling stuck with me the entire time.

One of my concerns about actually recreating what I did was how much my creativity and writing would suffer. It's hard to be sharp when you're tired. I'm sleepy as stuff right now. It feels like I'm just going through the motions. This might help with the constriction I was looking for. I felt that initially and at some points I was being long winded basically because I wanted to stretch this thing out but now that I'm nearing the end and know what I've said then it's like let me not bore you guys and just give you the details. People always ask me what I did while I was living on the streets and here's the skinny on that. The only obstacle was sleep and finding somewhere to charge my phone. I was apprehensive about sleeping outside so I just walked around all night. It killed time and kept me entertained. I'd walk up and down Hollywood blvd because as I found out, any other part of LA was barren at night. As far as charging my phone, I just had to come to terms with the fact that it would be dead for hours some nights.

There were places like Union Station, the Library and a few Fast Food places that had wall outlets I could abuse. I became the grand wizard of finding places to charge my phone. If there was an outlet to be found then I'd find it. Finding ways to inconspicuously catch up on sleep took more creativity. One of the things I would do was go in the restroom stalls at the gym, set my phone alarm for 20-25 minutes then sleep while sitting on the commode. Anything longer than that and I'm sure people would of thought I was dead. The library was a good napping ground just no the days when the security guards really cracked down on people sleeping in there. There was a couple instances when I'd get a lot of sleep done sitting at the tables in between the bookshelves. The first few days there I would ride the train or the bus and sleep on there but I stopped being able to afford it. That's how I ended up just walking around all night. It was free. The only cost was pain and discomfort. While I walked, I just kept telling myself that I only needed to make it to 5am. That was when Mcdowell's opened and I could go in there, relax and sneak in a short nap.

Seeing the sun coming up was my second wind. That second wind became harder to hold out for in those later days. Walking and the lack of sleep created this sort of odd vortex that I found myself in. Several times I blacked out while I was walking. I'd come to and wouldn't remember walking that far or even know where I was. Not only was I mentally defeated but I was physically defeated. My ankles and feet were always in pain. You would think a person would stop walking if they're in pain but the results of that would mean that I would collapse. That's the level of exhaustion I was at. I literally had to keep walking in order to keep myself awake. I didn't want to run the risk of falling asleep somewhere and something happening to me. If I sat down for even a second, I'd fall right to sleep, have to catch myself immediately, stand up and start back walking. The reason you see people talking to themselves isn't because they're crazy, it's because they're probably sleep deprived or so far removed from society that they just don't care. They're just trying to entertain themselves or have fell into this level of delusion. The same delusion I started to fall into. Those last few days, I became extremely delirious. I could just feel my sanity fading. I would do random things like smile or just yell for no reason. I began to talk to myself. I didn't feel like myself. I began to feel desperate to leave. That made the days feel longer and longer. I began to do random things like watching birds, singing to myself, dancing down the street and other things I wouldn't normally do just to help to pass the time. That veil of perception was fading away. I got comfortable wearing the same thing. I got comfortable not showering. I got comfortable with not eating. I got comfortable with not caring about my appearance. It was almost like for what? Who do I have to impress? I got comfortable letting my guards down and just accepting that this was my reality.

April 24th, 2010 was the first night I finally slept outside in the open! I was in Noho, I can't remember the street but I came across this cement ledge in front of this store. It was dark so I knew people walking wouldn't see me. So I tucked my shirt into my pants, tucked my pants into my socks to keep anything from crawling on my skin and laid down. I fell asleep immediately. Then things got a little sketchy. I woke up to the sound of a car pulling into the parking lot. It came right to where I was and stopped. The car only stayed for a few seconds then pulled off. Moments later the same car came back and pulled into the parking lot. This time a guy came from out of nowhere and got in the car, then they drove off. After they pulled off the I bolted from that place. Always the resourceful type, I ended up back on Hollywood Blvd, found a nice bus stop bench, laid down and fell asleep. It only lasted an hour but it felt like forever.

Fast forward to present day, I wanted and intended to recreate those last 10 days well, not recreate but put myself through a similar situation but it wouldn't be hard to do for me now. I'm virtual a LA transplant. Over the last few years, I visit here at least 5-6 times a year.I know my way around and know like 30 times more people than I knew then. Aside from that, my backpacking prowess is far superior now. I'm too savvy. Back then, I didn't utilize the places that are open 24 hours. I didn't consider places I utilize now to help kill time and take naps such as the airport or hospitals where I could go in at any time of day and sleep because who would know I'm not about to catch a flight or that I'm not in the waiting room visiting somebody. All things considered, I've decided to scrap that idea of trying to do things over again. That 26 year old version of me is dead and gone. The benefit of having content that's compelling for the book isn't motivation or incentive enough for me to subject myself to the sleep deprived thing. So, sorry folks. The blunt of those days are lost but I still have the timeline I was able to produce just based on my social media postings which is how I was able to know the date of my WORST night ever!!!!

April 26, 2010, I made the mistake of not getting back to the gym in time before they closed. One thing I don't think people realize about California is that it gets COLD there. There's no humidity there so nights are extremely chilly. My decision to wear only shorts and a T-shirt was fine during the day and ONLY during the day. The nights were too frigid. The wind didn't make matters pleasant. That night was horrible!!!!! I wanted to be anywhere but outside. Due to my limited options and the fact that my phone was dead, I think. I don't remember having it. As I write this I'm wondering why I didn't just call My Angel. There had to have been a good reason why I didn't. Maybe it was too late and I didn't feel like bothering her. I don't know. But I ultimately had no choice but to be outside. It was miserable. There was nothing to keep me warm. Nothing! I just had to suffer. While I was walking, I came across this little nook by the W off Hollywood blvd. There was this little makeshift cubby hole that was the entrance to a restaurant next to the hotel. I cornered myself in there and used on of those collapsible plastic sign they set outside of places to advertise their establishment, to box myself in and keep myself warm. The sign helped block the wind which offered some relief. I sat there and shivered, rubbing my hands together trying to generate some form of heat but couldn't. It was beyond frustrating. Mentally, I had to psyche myself out. I pulled my shirt over my knees, laid my head against the cement wall and slept for as long as I could.

Location: Los Angeles, CA
Date: April 23, 2016

Happy Birthday Lydia!!!! She's undoubtedly my favorite sister. We have such a funny bond. We text or talk almost everyday about funny things we remember from a movie or TV show we've seen. Some days she'll share with me how she's constipated or ask me weird scenarios like if I've ever been in the bathroom stall at work and have a person come in and be repulsed by the smell so you have to pull your feet back quickly hoping your co-worker doesn't see your shoes and call you out for what you've just done. What I realized was that all these scenarios she's asked were all first person accounts. Don't tell her I told you all that. LOVE YOU PUTHEAD!!!

As I mentioned earlier, I've been piecing together the rest of this book buy going through my social media posts to know what I did around the time I was in LA. I'm up to the point when I went to Skid Row for the first time on April 30th, 2010. I mentioned what that night was like. It was like 120 pages ago, you can flip back and refresh your mind if you want to, I'll wait. See it? Great. What I want to know is how many of you have been to Skid Row? Are you all aware that in a major city within the United States that there are hundreds of people living and sleeping on the streets on a daily basis and it's been occurring for well over 20 years? How did these people get here? Why is this ok?

It still angers me to this day. What angers me most is that I passed through that area the other day and it still exists!!!!!!!!!!!!!! They've built new buildings and lofts all around so that much has changed. My friend told me that they're slowly building up that area to improve the property value. So, since people living on the street brings down the property value, let's build condos and lofts to bring money to the area. Genius! That sounds very practical I must admit but what about those people on the streets? What is being built for them? I feel the same way about Skid Row that I feel about women becoming strippers or prostitutes, it shouldn't even be an option. There are always better ways to be effective in society. These things shouldn't be in place or even be an option for people to do. No knock against strippers or women who are prostitutes but it's troubling that we're part of a society where money is enough to make people expose themselves strictly for sexual purposes. That isn't right. I think is a horrible facet to society. I cringe at the thought of having a daughter in this world when the "sex sells" mantra is so prevalent. That's another story for another book. I will say this, Women should be respected and highly regarded. Women should not feel they have to lower their self worth to get ahead in the world. That's not a bad notion right? Aside from that, I feel we need to put more effort and emphasis into correcting the poverty level in society. I'm not one of those people who feel like you should give people handouts but you should offer help to those who will take that help and do something with it. Let's be honest, some of the people who are homeless are a lost cause but there are people who are only homeless do in part to circumstances out of their control. (ie Loss of employment, loss of property, and for not having a support system)

On two occasions since I've been here in LA I've tried to give shoes to a couple of guys I saw walking barefoot. They both declined. In their mind they're far removed from the normal ideas of comfort. If you go so long without something you forget what it's like to have it. There have been times when I offered people money and they've declined. Not sure if they declined out of pride or just didn't need the use of money. When I was living on the street, I came across several people of sound mind and body who were homeless. I remember this one kid on Hollywood Blvd who was holding a sign saying he just needed money to get back home. Not sure if that was a ploy but he definitely looked as if he'd be living on the streets for a while.

The term "homeless" is so relative. To me, homeless just means that you don't own a place to live. That's the most technical and literal definition of it to me. When I tell people I'm homeless they assume that I'm broke, dusty, sleep in a cardboard box and dig in the trash. That is one form of the characteristics associated with being homeless but it's not all of them. Why is digging in the trash even an option? In college when I worked at Mcdowell's, I would close most nights and every single night we would count "waste." Waste was food that fell on the floor as well as things not edible but the bulk of it was just leftover food. Food that didn't sell. One night I asked the manager why can't we just take this food that we're literally throwing into the trash and give it to homeless people? She explained to me that there's some sort of liability that would come with that. For that fact the company wouldn't be willing to risk it. Like ok, let's not feed hungry people just in case one of them get sick from it and therefore tries to sue? Got it. That was just one store, think about it on a national scale of how much food gets tossed in the trash daily. If you were to ask me how the world works then I'd have ZERO input to offer. One thing I will say that I've noticed about the world is that it's selfish. It seems like everybody is out for self and only see ways to make their life better. Living on the street made me more self aware and mindful of others. It's hard for me to walk past a homeless person and not give them money.

Money in my opinion is the easiest commodity to attain. It's in abundance.There's no signs that say conserve money. Only signs that say conserve energy and water. They've made all these cost efficient products while the price of everything continues to soar. I went in the grocery and aside for some fruit and candy, there's nothing that you can buy for a dollar. In my youth I used to eat like a king for $3. In LA, the minimum wage is expected to rise to $15/hr. It's concerning to realize that the cost of living is rapidly increasing but the cost of others living is declining. Where's the compassion? Not once have I walked through LA and NYC and said to myself. *"You know what, this place needs more buildings and high rise lofts"* Not once. As I walked through NYC two weeks ago and around LA the other day. That's all I seen. New construction. You know what else I seen when I was in NYC? People living on the streets.

There was one lady in particular laying on the sidewalk with a blanket on. It was 30 degrees!! Before 2010, I would walk by these same people and wonder to myself what's it's like to do that. So when people ask why would I want to subject myself to 26 days of living on the street. That's why. That's why I did it. I'm no better than that woman. I'm no better than any of these people. We're all just one wrong decision or unfortunate scenario from being just like them. Nobody rows up and say hey I want to let drugs or alcohol ruin my life. Nobody grows up saying I want to run away from home as a teenager then spend the rest of my life living on the street. Nobody decides their life. We're given choices. Sometimes those choices are wise and sometimes those choices have an everlasting affect on us. Both good and bad. My journey broadened my perspective on the aspect of living on the streets. It also broadened my perspective on how messed up this world is. Not sure who said this but "Sometimes it's not about changing, it's about adapting" My adaptation was a 26 day process. I adapted to the concept of "less is more." If I can make it 26 days with just two pair of pants and whatever else I had in my backpack, then why can't that be an everyday thing? If I can get by with sleeping on the bus, train or at a friends house here and there then why can't that be an everyday thing? Ultimately, what is the good of solely having material possessions?

Remember when I was trying to figure out what to pack before I went to LA? It happened about 130 pages ago, you can flip back and refresh your mind if you want to. I'll wait. See it? Great! The inventory in my backpack right now is: 1 pair of soccer pants, 3 pairs of basketball shorts, 3 T-shirts, 5 pairs of socks, a windbreaker and my running shoes. What I didn't know back then was that I'd spend the next 6 years ultimately living out a backpack. Why? FREEDOM.

Freedom afforded to me because I decided not to work endless hours for a company and corporation where the CEO owns a private jet while the people who work for them catch the bus or gets rides there. I'd rather be that CEO who catches the bus with the workers. Success is attainable to us all and if you work hard to get yourself a jet then by all means get yourself a jet. Me personally, I'd never own a jet, an expensive piece of jewelry or an expensive car. I don't see the point. I had a conversation with somebody about how insane it is that people will purchase a watch for the price of $40,000.There are people who don't even make 40k/yr. Put that into perspective. Somebody is working hard 40 hours a week for 52 for that 40k/yr salary and there are people who spend that on one purchase. Such a disparity. I'm not sure how to bridge the gap but please don't be that person making 40k/year doing something you don't love to do. Otherwise you're cheating yourself.

They always say if you're not part of the solution then you're part of the problem. It took me no time to realize that I can't change the world. I just decided not to be of the world. In no way am I saying living out of a backpack is the new life craze or that everybody should jump on board because it's definitely not for everybody. What I am saying is that I hope that with the creation of this book I find out I'm not the only one. The term "nomad" exist so I'm sure in that regard but if I'm not the only one doing for the reasons I decided to do it. I might be the only one. I'm eager to find out if there are other people with a similar train of thought. Everything in life needs structure, I'm not anti the structure of the world in it's entirety, just the part that involves me being apart of the structure. It's a great structure because everything relies on other people and other entities to make one thing. One of the things I've done on the side is work on construction sites doing general labor. What's fascinating is that it takes at least 10-20 different companies just to build something. It takes factories to make the products, companies to make the product that the factories makes, delivery companies to deliver the product. It the equipment used to build the product. A company to make the equipment used to build the product. The people designing the product. The people who make the tools that designers use to create the product on. The contractors who build it. The separate companies that will do HVAC, electricity, windows, plumbing, painting and flooring. There's so many different moving parts. The world is the same way, people profit off of every aspect in life. Death is a profitable business, can you imagine how business meetings at a funeral home goes? "We had a good year this year, profits are up. Good job guys!" This girl I know used to be a news reporter. She quit because of how consuming it became. She was a field reporter and as you know on the news the things most mentioned are tragedies. After a few years, covering deaths, missing kids, house fires and gang shootings really takes it's tole on a person.

Life took it's tole on me. I just needed a break. I just needed my freedom. I just needed to not be affected by the world. I find it to be so peaceful. If you had to ask me what stress or feeling worried feels like then I wouldn't know how to describe it. I'm a big ball of positive vibes and happy feelings. Being alone is the best feeling ever. Not having to appease others or worry about what others think is empowering! I'm grateful that I don't have to go to a job that I hate. That I can pick and choose when I want to work. That I don't have to put up with individuals and compromise who I am. This allows me to be 100% myself. There was this movie I watched the other day called "Lucy" (which was an awful movie by the way). The movie is about this girl who was able to use a higher percentage of her brain than normal humans can. Due to this, she developed this supreme level of knowledge that was like super powers. I'm not using more of my brain but I am able to cut out the undo stress of life. Unlike her, I can't move things with my mind or see through buildings but I can see the world from a totally different aspect. It makes me feel like I'm looking at a whole new world. Often times it's like, *"Am I the only person who can see this?"* It's rare that I find people who can grasp the concept of what I'm doing. There are others who think it's pretty freaking awesome that I can travel literally all the time without worrying about PTO or having to be back at work on Monday. The first time I ever went on a plane was when I was 25-ish. Since then I've caught over a hundred flights. Aside from 12-ish states, I've been all over the country. One time last year I had sat and calculated the number of miles I had traveled in the past 2 months. I forget the number but it was like 55k miles or something crazy like that. The million dollar question people ask when they notice how much I travel is *"Are you rich?" "How can you afford to travel so much?" "What do you do for a living?"* Those questions annoy me because they're asked with interest of if there's something to gain from me. They wonder if I can pay for their flights or if I know how to get them free flights. It's possible that you were thinking the very same thing. Some of you are genuine and have wondered the same thing without the angle of trying to get something out of me. Since I'm in a good mood I'll tell you how I'm able to afford it. I'm homeless. Money is the easiest commodity to attain but it's not the most valuable.

Time is.

I have literally nothing but free time. The people who have the money to travel, don't have the time. The people who have the time to travel, don't have the money. My bills for the month come up to a whopping total of $134 bucks. That includes my phone bill and gym membership which is really like my rent. I have the membership where I can go to any Louisville Fitness in the country. They're in every major city so I enjoy those perks of always having a pace to store my belongings, shower and kill time no matter where I go. Without having to pay rent, insurance or whatever bills you people have to pay. The money I make all goes to catching one way flights. There's an art to getting good flights. Majority of the flights are cheapest when it's just one way or when you plan on traveling during the week. Booking 3 weeks to a month in advance gets you the lowest prices. Majority of the flight I catch are less than $100 bucks unless I'm flying cross country then at most it'll be $150. Between some cities I've caught fights for as low as $25 For most people, If they look up a flight, it's either during the weekend or around holidays so naturally those are going to be higher ticket prices because the airlines know that's when people are more likely prone to fly. That's Economics 101. I don't have the money to fly, but I have the time to fly. My other means of traveling is by bus. In the Northeast, some of those trips are as little as $14

Traveling really isn't expensive for me I just have to get there. I don't have to pay for a hotel or rent a car. I crash with friend's or family or just sleep in the airport overnight. I have a horrible diet so I don't have to spend much money on food. I don't eat fast food anymore but I can go without eating real food. Take this week for instance, aside from yesterday when I had chicken strips two sides and a biscuit for $5 bucks, my intake has been water, juice, chips, fries, one chicken taco, 1 chicken dumpling, cookies, plain bagels, candy. That's it. And as you can tell none of that stuff is expensive. The other day I ran 5 miles then played pickup basketball for 2 hours. Ask me what all did I eat that day. Chips and Gatorade. People who know of my eating habits love to tell me how unhealthy I am and how I need to change but it's not something that I need to change because it's something I've already adapted to.

When I joined the Air Force in 2013-ish, I got a physical and you know what the Dr told me? That at age 29, I was in perfect health. This was after a time of several years when my diet revolved around eating whole packs of cookies. I'd literally just eat nothing but cookies, I'd eat a pack a day and nothing else majority of the time. The military changed that habit quickly. In basic training we weren't allowed to get desserts. Allegedly. What I realized later is that we were allowed but that it was frowned upon. Some trainees were bold enough to put a dessert or pop on their tray. It was always funny to be in the DFAC and have those poor innocent first weekers come out of the food line with a pop or a dessert and walk in front of the "Snake pit". The "Snake Pit" was the table were all the high ranking MTI's sat. They would literally just sit there and pick out trainees to call over to the table and ask questions and yell at you if you didn't know something or that you would DARE enjoy a carbonated beverage and a dessert when you're training to be part of the military. Oh, I guess now would be a good time to talk about how I joined the Air Force eh? Well we haven't got to that part in the story yet but it'll come. Before we get to that, let me talk about my immediate depression after returning back to "Society" after those 26 days.

I've heard accounts of how people who return home from prison or war have trouble adapting back into society. By no terms was my 26 days anything like war or prison but similar in the sense that I had to attempt to try to fit back into society. I didn't. But that doesn't mean that I never tried. Once I got back to Atlanta, I went right back to working at Target, listened to stories of who quit, who got fired, who transferred, who got caught stealing, who was dating who and hadn't every minute of it. I just didn't care to be there. It wasn't refreshing, I had to deal with people. One thing I learned about myself in recent years is that I don't like people. Aside from my disdain for people, a lot of things changed after I got back. If you can recall my levels of trust were already low so imagine returning back to a life you left and that life not being there. Imagine you placed your glasses down, left the room, then came back and your glasses were gone.

"Who in the hell moved my glasses?"

You continually ask and nobody seems to know. This forces you to become more and more irate. You have to look at everybody in the room as if somebody is lying. They know who the h*ll moved your d*mn glasses but they're conspiring against you to keep you oppressed and not let you see things clearly. That's the metaphor to how my life was those few weeks after I got back. The most important thing to me was this girl who I had felt showed me love. I had been confident that that love would still be there. It wasn't. It hurts being lied to. It tears your trust to shreds. It hurts even more when you went through what I went through. They say you shouldn't make expectations. I've since ceased those practices but I expected so much and got so little. I expected some reprieve. I expected the life I left to still be there. It wasn't. Imagine expecting a welcome banner and all you get is a text. 26 days living on the street makes a man highly vulnerable and paranoid. That pain was unbearable. This made me volatile. This made me an emotional wreck.

This made me lose whatever trust I had left. Again I was blindsided by reality. It was like being 24 all over again, realizing that there were still more facades left. Just imagine if Truman walked through that door and into what he deemed "The Real World" only to realize 2 years later that that was just another set opposite the one he just got away from. I was overwhelmed. I panicked, in my mind I just felt like everybody was against me and nobody sympathized with what I had just went through and expected too much from me. In a moment of paranoia and anxiety I walked out of my sister's apartment to the lake behind her complex and chucked my phone into the water.

It was at that moment I found peace. It was in that moment that I found freedom. It was in that moment I took control of my life and decided that I won't let anything or anyone dictate my joy. A wise man once told me "*He who angers you, owns you*" Nobody owns me. Expectations are for lazy people. I decided to not expect things but to create the things I wanted. To not rely on others but to do things myself. Compromise is necessary but in that moment I decided to never compromise the things I believe in. That I won't let anything or anyone dictate my life. This is my life. This is my destiny. I don't owe anybody any explanations. Some people will get it. Some people won't. To the people on the fence, I'll leave you this:

You ain't around me everyday so you don't know my life
the pain or stress I feel and what that's like
but I'll expose my soul a little and give you some insight
I won't admit to being wrong but I ain't always right
I've laughed more than I've cried
but frowned more than I've smiled
been up then down
can't say I enjoyed that ride
The tears I hide...

Let me tell you why I'm this way hold

These street signs and buildings look familiar. I've been on this road before. Seems just like yesterday I was 6 years old bouncing my basketball up and down the sidewalks of Village West Apartments. As long as the weather permitted, there I was. Outside. Dribbling. The sound echoed from the early mornings until the late evenings when the street lights began to illuminate the night skies. Periodically I'd glance up to the second floor window of our apartment and see the face of my mother looking back at me. She would peer through the windows just to confirm my presence. Other times she'd open the front door and peer left and right to see where I was if I had strayed out of the eyeline sight of the window. I never went too far. However, my imagination took me everywhere. It had too. Reality was never my friend. It feels better to envision better days than to deal with the harsh truths. The harsh truths of growing up in poverty. Growing up without confidence. Growing up terrified by your own insecurities. Bullied by your own fears. Misguided by the perceptions of others. Bottled up with anger, resentment, mistrust and confusion. Why us? Why me? It's hard for a child to amass answers to the things they don't understand. It takes years before they even began to question things. I wasn't like most children. It was an immediate observation that certain things shouldn't be omitted from my life. My mother says I was always inquisitive since an early age and would always ask "*Why?*" I pleaded for knowledge. I pleaded for understanding. Things just didn't seem fair. My inquisitive persona forged my desire to find out things for myself and learn on my own. I instinctively felt like something was wrong. Why was it wrong? Why didn't we have the things the kids at my school had? Why were we on food stamps? Why didn't my mom or dad ever go to work? Why did I primarily get hand me downs from my brothers and cousin but never got items purchased directly for me? Why? Why? Why? I'd ask my mother and she'd explain things to me the best she could. One thing she never explained was that not being normal or typical wasn't a bad thing.

On my first day of headstart, I remember eating lunch. I had only been there half a day. My mom comes and tells me, "*...let's go.*" I didn't know what happened, I thought I had done something wrong. So I asked her "*What did I do?*" She replied "*Nothing baby, you don't have* *to be here. They want to send you right to kindergarten."* At 4 years old, I didn't notice the difference in me being different. To me, I felt being different was a bad thing. My clothes looked different. My shoes looked different. My skin looked different. My hair looked different. Being in a "special" class, didn't make me feel special. It made me feel isolated. Being intellectual is something I should of been proud of but it just got the ball rolling on my insecurities and feelings of not fitting in. For the bulk my academic career, my peers were nothing like me. They were all from suburban households. They would bring lunch to school and talk of things I never knew existed. Such as having a house and a yard. Having multiple cars. Having their own room. Getting an allowance. Things common to most was uncommon to me. Why wasn't my life comparable to those I spent the bulk of my days with? It's astonishing how you're so unaware of the things you lack until you're made aware of them. It was never apparent to me that living in government housing wasn't normal. It was never apparent to me that sharing a room with two siblings wasn't normal. It was never apparent that I wasn't on a equal playing field. The people around you are your reflections. They're there to show you your life and make you aware. There was never a time I was teased for being on free lunch. There was never a time when I was teased for wearing my brother's clothes to school. There was never a time I was teased for my family being lower class. Nobody made me feel bad about it except for myself. It made me feel secluded. It made me feel inadequate. It made me associate that blame to my parents. Why did they allow this to happen? Why? Those answers never were answered. I felt it up to myself to fix it. I felt it up to myself to dream of making millions so that I could escape.

My obsession became the dire need to improve my surroundings. That's why I dribbled that basketball. That's why I made good grades. That's why I worked hard to be the best at whatever I did. That fire inside fueled me to push myself. It's not where you're from, it's where you end up. We started off at a disadvantage so we had to take advantage of our lives and aim high. To reach the top, we had to dream bigger. We had to evolve. I evolved. I vowed to be better. To let nothing of my present represent my past. There are some things you never forget and some things that you never get over. It's almost like at some point you just learn to accept them. I've accepted my insecurities but the process of doing so didn't happen overnight. Some of those insecurities still linger in the back of my mind.

Homosexuality was one of those insecurities. Even to this day, it's still an insecurity. Something that I used to ask myself was *"Am I gay?"* If I had declared that I was gay how would I go about expressing it? In the devout christian household I grew up in, we were told homosexuality was an abomination. It wasn't tolerated. It wasn't an option. That being said, imagine the pure rage and anger in my father's eyes as he walked into his room and saw his nephew and 8 year old son standing wearing one of his wife's dresses. The quote: *"God made Adam and Eve not Adam and Steve"* was drilled into my head that entire evening. Prayers were prayed. Discipline was delivered. The truth is that I didn't put on that dress because I wanted to look like woman. I did it because my cousin did it. I honestly didn't know better. For years I had to deal with the insecurities of others thinking I was gay. For years I had to deal with fears of what being gay meant and how I could shake from it. My siblings did an amazing job of helping to cloud my psyche. They repeatedly taunted me. Initially, it was because of my speech impediment because I used to have a horrible stuttering problem and had to go to speech class every morning before school. There are words I still can't pronounce properly, anything with a "str" like *street* or *straight,* I couldn't pronounce correctly if you put a gun to my head. It it wasn't that then it was because at my age I still hd issues with wetting the bed. Something that I didn't overcome until I was 14-ish. My brothers and sisters graciously eased up from taunting me about those things in exchange for taunting me with lovely homophobic slurs and anything other form or reference of calling me gay they could come up with. It took me years to even determine if I was gay or not.. I tried my hardest not to be gay. I wasn't sure if I was suppressing it until it was accepting to admit it or if I was truly not gay. Growing up as an adolescent constantly bombarded by accusations of homosexual behaviors forces one to second guess themselves. They called me gay so much that I used to think to myself that maybe I am gay. I was constantly self aware of how I'd be perceived and conscious not to do or say things that would make people think I was gay. It didn't work. People still found reasons to assume that I might be gay. Routinely I was made fun of because of my voice and how it "sounded gay" and prodded with things such as "put some bass in your voice". I used to hate talking on the phone because people would think I was a girl. Even to this day I don't like talking on the phone subconsciously for the same reason. Sure, I have more bass in my voice but now instead of sounding like a girl, I get told that I sound like a kid who just went through puberty. Homosexuality to me back then didn't mean having sex with a man, it meant not being tough enough. It meant being weak, being picked on and treated like a girl. I had to fight to distance myself from that stigma. I had try to prove my toughness. There weren't many days that went by that I didn't get into a fist fight. Not because I wanted to. Because I had to. Running from a fight or getting beat up was a no no. I didn't need others having any more ammunition to belittle me with so I fought. Fighting brought respect. It's how I proved to others that I wasn't weak. That I wasn't a pushover. That I wasn't a punk. That I wasn't a wuss. More importantly, to prove that I wasn't gay.

Homosexual accusations aside, there were other insecurities I fought against. I wasn't the most svelte of kids. I was still carrying my baby fat and the bulk of that baby fat was in my chest. Going swimming meant leaving my shirt on. I used to wear multiple shirts just to hide them. My teeth, which were described as appearing to look like a crowd of people running towards an exit, was something else I was self conscious about I used to make sure to laugh and use my hand to cover my mouth. There were literally teeth growing from my gums on top of other teeth. We couldn't afford braces and years went by before I got my baby teeth pulled. I used to get called "count dracula" or "shark teeth".There was always something about me that people pointed out and made me aware of. Physically I knew I'd never gain confidence so I focused on what I could be confident about, sports and being on the honor roll. I was constantly trying to find ways to value my worth. I was constantly trying to overcome these insecurities. I was constantly in search of trying to find validation. I was constantly in search of trying to find myself. With each dribble, with each bounce, my search intensified. Right hand. Let hand. Behind the back. Through the legs. Shoot. Swish. My premiere escape from everything was basketball. No matter what, as long as my ball had air, I had something to do. Somewhere to go. Didn't matter the day, the year, the weather or how early the time of day.

My sanctuary was whereever my basketball took me. There was zero doubt in my mind that this would be my way out. It wasn't.

During my journey in LA, I realized that regrets are a symbol of being ungrateful. Everything it took me to get to this person I am now is by design. Not being rich used to be a regret of mine. Not furthering my basketball dreams used to be a regret of mine. There were a ton of decisions and things I did over the course of my life that were regrettable if I allowed myself to think in that manner. I don't. When people associate words like cocky and arrogant to describe my self love and confidence, I don't get it. My love and appreciation for myself and my life doesn't come from a superficial aspect. I'm still that soft voice, bad acne, crooked teeth, poor kid with man boobs. Sure when others look at me they see this tall, insanely handsome, charismatic debonair gentleman but just know that that's just the top layer. I wasn't who I was before I got here. It took time. It took a chain of events. It took me growing up.

In the summer of 1995-ish, My family and I moved from Village West into a three story house into a middle class neighborhood located in the Shively area of Louisville, KY. That following Fall, I entered the 6th grade at Noe Middle School. Unlike Grade School, Noe had a basketball team and I set my sights on claiming the spot reserved for me. I had began playing organized basketball around the age of around 5 or 6-ish in this basketball league called "Hot Shots" every Saturday. Speaking humbly, I was a phenomenon. I'm sure you all can guess what I did in that league:

GET BUCKETS!

All that practice, all those games feeling dominant playing with"Hot Shots" gave me an inflated ego. An ego that fully deflated once I tried out for the 6th grade team at Noe and didn't make it. This was a pivotal moment in my life. Sure the disappointment was daunting but the value I learned was that things never go as planned. Nobody is going to hand you anything and you'll never receive anything you don't deserve. You have to work hard if you want to be successful. When my name wasn't called as part of the players who made team, it was awkward. It didn't immediately register. I didn't immediately understand the significant life goals being laid out.

During the beginning of my 6th grade year, I found out something unexpected about myself. I found out that I really loved music! Learning something new was exciting. What was even more exciting was that we were allowed to take our instruments home with us. After a few weeks, as I continued to improve, I would divide my time between practicing on my trumpet and playing basketball in the driveway. My love for basketball never diminished but not playing basketball gave me that entire year to focus on playing the trumpet. Before the end of the year I had made it to first chair in the band. My competitive nature transferred from the hardwood to the band room. Just as hard as I pushed myself by dribbling and shooting for hours, I pushed myself just as hard by learning to read notes and play music. Something else the absence of basketball helped me notice was the absence of my father.

It was around this point in my life tenure that I began to notice a common thread. A trend. Where was my Father? Unlike most of the kids in Village West, my dad was there, he actually lived with us. Periodically. My mom and dad would argue which led to him being kicked out the house for a few months. He'd be reduced to pulling up outside. We would all go out to the car talk to him and carry in the bags of groceries he had bought. Growing up in a predominantly black neighborhood, having your dad around meant you were rich. There were numerous times when other kids were shocked to not only find out that I know who my dad is but that my parents were also married. My parents have maintained their dysfunctional relationship for almost 40 years now. That's the only form of what love is that I know. No matter what they say or do to each other their love is a bond that's unbreakable and that's a beautiful thing. They made vows and continue to honor them. Cheers to them.

The older I got I finally began to realize that the dysfunction was happening before my eyes and used to try to rationalize to myself *"Why do they yell at each other?" "Why do they say these things to each other" "Why is he always packing up his clothes and leaving just to come back a few days or weeks later? "Why does my mom always talk about him beating on her?"* I personally never witnessed my father strike my mother but I wondered about the validity of these claims. Never did I witness physical violence but I did witness psychological violence. For some reason, my mother had this pension for attempting to jump out of the car whenever my dad and her argued in the car. Why would she want to harm herself? I never realized the dynamic of their relationship or exactly how flawed it was. It seemed normal. It was a routine. No matter what they never stopped loving each other. They were husband and wife but more importantly they were parents, My dad was physically there but it's hard to say his presence was impressionable in the raising and development of a young man. My dad served as the disciplinarian. In all honesty, my mother potentially deserved blame for some of the faults I noticed in my childhood but I never blamed her. She was always there to love me. I remember in kindergarten buying her this green pocket mirror. It's the same green pocket mirror that she still carries in her purse 26 years later. In those 26 years she's the only person that has loved me unconditionally. The only person who believed in me nonstop. The only person who trusted that no matter what I was going to do the right thing. Sure she had concerns about my path and some decisions I've made along the way but she never let it interfere with her love for me and how much she believed in me. There's nothing greater than a mother's love. The love of my mother gets me through a lot of days. It gives me strength that no matter what, there's always going to be at least one person in my corner. My mother always give me positive reinforcement and encouragement. She gets complete credit for my ability to be creative, for my instinctive care and compassion for others as well as my ambition. She supported anything I did. Would it had been too much for me to expect that same support from both parents? My mom was the nurturer. She'd discipline us occasionally but nothing more than a quick slap or arm pinch. My mom was the hugger, the kisser, the motivator, the person who'd give you pep talks and always encourage us to be better and to strive to succeed. My pops was was from the old school back when it wasn't taboo to use objects to discipline your offsprings. His tools of discipline altered between a belt and a switch, both of which he used masterfully with amazing accuracy and precision. Discipline is necessary so I never regret any of it nor do I fault my pops for how he conducted business. I just wish there was a better balance of discipline and teaching your son to be a man. The beauty was that I was able to use his discipline to become a man.

There are two profound disciplinary instances during my 6th grade year that I'll never forget. They pinpoint the moment in life when I began to mature into my own individual. The first particular incident occurred after my teacher called home to inform my mom that I was having trouble staying focused in classes. My sister Lydia still brings up this event whenever she can because while getting a whooping, my father had me repeat what he said, much like parents of those days did. I think. Or maybe my dad was a mold all his own. Either way. As he whooped me, he made me repeat whatever he said. One of those phrases was, "I'm going to behave, in all classes." It should be pointed out that my dad's deductive reasoning wasn't the best. When experiencing pain, your enunciation is liable to suffer. My delivering of the end of the phrase "in all classes" wasn't sufficient enough so he whooped me while telling me to repeat it three additional times. That became the sound bite that Lydia and my siblings heard the loudest and for years have repeated it to me because I literally had to yell it to get away from proceeding to have thin slivers of wood slash across my shirtless body.

The second occurrence came a few month later. It was the last whopping I ever go. I'm not sure what I did or didn't do to warrant this whooping but I went about things different. I knew it was coming. I went into it fearless. Confident. As a man, you take your punishment. That's what I did. My father sat with me and talked to me and allowed me to explain myself and the incident that occurred. It gave me some false assurance like maybe I'm not going to get a whooping this time. After about 30-45 minutes. The gauntlet came down and the courts had ruled guilty and thus sentenced to immediate punishment. The boys always had to take our shirts off when we got whoopings, However, this time, My father requested that I removed all items of clothing. After he left the room to retrieve his tools I sat there, waiting. I wasn't concerned, worried or fearful. My dad returned, having time to reevaluate things he told me to put my clothes back on. In my mind, by not showing fear, I was being defiant, this was me confronting my father and showing him I no longer feared him. When I began to think back and question where my father was. I realized he was never there in the capacity I felt like he should have been. Why was I dribbling and shooting by myself? Why was I falling off my bike trying to learn by myself? Why was I tying my shoes by myself? Why was I getting into fights by myself? Why was Lavon teaching me how to tie a tie? Why was I doing so many things by myself with no fatherly guidance or warranted advice? It became apparent to me that my father wasn't there for me. My father didn't raise me. My father didn't bring value. His role was that of obedience. His role was fear. Discipline. What he says goes. Only his thoughts and words mattered. There was never any room to have a voice. There was never any room to be your own individual. As I sat there naked waiting for him to come back, I grew angered. It was embarrassing. *"Why was he going to such advanced measures to discipline me?"* I asked myself. There was rage in my eyes. After getting dressed, I assumed that he had noticed my rage and noticed how I sat there without fear. The fear he had seen and expected me to have. I purposely sat with great posture in anticipation of whatever punishment occurred. Me getting dressed wasn't his way of sparing me. As it turns out, I still got a whopping. The difference was that there was no call and response. There was no tears. I didn't cry. I stood there and absorbed the pain. Mentally, I knew that I couldn't show pain. Mentally, I understood that psychologically I could fight back. Physically, I couldn't. Our relationship disintegrated progressively from that moment on. In turn, I progressively found out more about myself and the person I was becoming.

During the summer of 1997, my family and I moved to a brand new house in the West End of Louisville KY. That was the good news. The bad news was that due to our change of address I'd have to transfer schools. Bummer. Based on the zoning, which determines which schools kids are allowed to go, Noe wasn't in the zone of our house. My "home school" was Kammerer Middle School, a school in the suburban East End of Louisville. Changing school was devastating to me for one reason and one reason only. Nia. She was my first love. Well, she was the first girl I felt I loved. She was the first girl I wrote love letters to and love notes about. Thanks to the radio, music heavily influenced my life and helped paint my thoughts and perception of what I perceived love to be. My favorite artist around that time was K. Relly. I would sit in my room all evening listening to his self titled album "K. Relly" and write her love letters. Aaliyah's song "4 page letter" was to blame for my young impressionable mind thinking that the best way to prove your love was to literal write 4 page letters. Much like I did with basketball and playing the trumpet, I pushed myself to write the best love letters ever. Nia would read my letters and tell me how good they were.This was when I realized that I enjoyed creating and being able to convey my thoughts by using words.

My first unofficial introduction to writing was in 4th grade. While attending Coleridge Taylor Elementary School. We had to do these writing portfolios that required us to submit short stories and other literary entries. The first story I penned was entitled "The Magic Pencil" which was about an misfortunate kid from a very poor family. His family couldn't afford to buy him nice clothes and in school he was picked on because of it. While on his way home from school one day, he comes across an old raggedy pencil. Everybody has walked past the pencil without ever thinking to pick it up. When he sees the pencil, he sees it as something he could use. He picked it up and carried it home.. Later that evening he realized that the pencil possessed good luck and fortune. With this pencil he developed the ability to wish for all the things he ever wanted. He used those wishes to help his family and all of those less fortunate. My teacher at the time informed me of how much she enjoyed my writing and insisted that I continue to write. After reading my completed writing portfolio she asked me where my imagination came from. My imagination came from my dreams of escaping my reality. It's better to dream than it is to lie awake. It's better to believe in having redemption. Sometimes it's better to pretend that things have changed, in hopes that maybe one day they will. We all desire improvements.

One thing I intended to improve upon was my disappointment of not making the basketball team at Noe. Leading up to tryouts at Kammerer, I spent hours and hours outside playing and practicing on my basketball hoop that my father had bought me for me a year prior. Our new house didn't have a driveway so I had to wheel my basketball goal to this vacant lot on the other side of our neighbors house. With more adequate space. My talent advanced. It was now time for the moment of truth. During tryouts, in order to differentiate one team from the other we played "shirts and skins" One team wore shirts while the other team had to take their shirts off and be "skins". The first two days I dodged that bullet of being skins. The last day I wasn't so fortunate. Soon as I took my shirt off, all the other kids burst out with laughter. One kid yelled "*He got titties!!*" The taunts and insults hurt but they fueled me to be the best player with titties ever! Laughs wouldn't and couldn't stop me from what I did during tryouts:

GET BUCKETS!

To no surprise, I made the team and became a fixture in history as our 7th and 8th grade basketball team went undefeated, which capped off 3 consecutive undefeated seasons.

The summer going into my first year of High School I was obsessed with reforming my body. For me, I determined the best way to do this was to get a 6 pack. I spent every night in bed doing crunches while listening to music. I treated that just as I treated basketball, playing the trumpet and writing: I pushed myself and worked hard to improve. I showed up to 9th grade year with a perfectly sculpted 6 pack and guess what else. Titties! What became apparent to me was that I didn't have man boobs but that I had a deformity. My brothers and I all share the same affliction. No matter what, that excess flesh in our chest area is here to stay. As my man boobs stayed my love and passion for basketball faded.

My Junior year at Ballard High School was another turning point in the maturation process of my life. My love and appreciation for basketball had begun to deteriorate. Our team was ranked 3rd in the nation that year but this time, being part of a dynasty began to not work in my favor. There was a pecking order. I was good but I wasn't as good as others on our team. Our starting 5 all received scholarships to Division 1 schools so that shows the level of talent I was up against. I could have transferred to lesser schools to get more shine like some other kids did but I didn't want to. I liked where I was. After deciphering my dad's psychological tactics, I became a less impressionably individual and thus my resistance to structure, being controlled or manipulated intensified. At Ballard it felt like it was more about money than it was about talent. In a couple of cases, money dictated who made the team. If your Mom or Dad worked at the school determined who made the team. If your parent was a booster determined who made the team. This didn't sit well from me. The kids who looked like me and had superior talent were overlooked in favor of the kid whose parent was at every practice, at every game or whose dad was apart of the coaching staff. My junior year this affected me directly. To make the varsity team we were required to run a mile in under 6 minutes; something I struggled to do. It wasn't until my "make or break" moment, well into the start of the season that two of my coaches took me to this indoor track at Southeast Christian Church with the ultimatum of "if you make the time, you're on the team, if you don't, then you're off the team" Every lap was a time spent deep in thought, focused on the task at hand. One of our assistant coaches kept track of my time and with each lap he'd yell out my current time and the pace I needed to maintain in order to make the time. My coach did me the biggest favor ever. Instead of telling me the exact time he would add 5 seconds to the time of my actual pace so that I knew I had to maintain the same speed or else I wouldn't make the time. This forced me to continue to push myself and ignore my desires to quit. When I finally completed the grueling required laps to complete 1 mile, Coach told me my time. 5 minutes 31 seconds! With that monkey off my back I knew the rest of the year would be smooth sailing.

Every year the varsity basketball team takes a trip during the Winter time to play a Holiday tournament. This year was no difference. It was a trip I had looked forward to going to since my Freshman year. One day before the trip was coming up my coaches informed me that my spot for that trip had been given away because they never expected me to run the mile successfully. Gee. Thanks. Who did my spot go to? A sophomore whose parents were boosters. Despite my disappointment, I didn't quit the team, that year. My Senior year, I wasn't so forgiving. Before the last day of tryouts my coach brought me and two other individuals into his office to inform us that we were all competing for the last spot of the team. Instantly I thought to myself "*The what? Last spot on the huh??*" This enraged me. The two players next to me weren't as half as good as me. In all honesty, I was probably one of if not thee most talented person on that team that year. But it wasn't about talent, it was about money. Before that final day of tryouts, I had made up my mind and said to myself to hell with this team. I wanted to let my action dictate the words I couldn't really express. I wanted to go out in grand fashion and inform the masses of the poor decisions being levied against me. I used a particular one on one drill we did in try-outs to drive this point home. The drill was that we played one on one while the others waited in line. The person who scored first stayed on the court. The other player had to fall back in line. Then the next player up. Once I got on the court, I never got off the court. I just wanted to show how insulting it was to even put me in that position. To show that I was better than what they took me for. To show that I can't be controlled. That I can't be manipulated. That fair is fair and wrong is wrong. I understand that in certain cases you have to compromise to get along with others. I'm not completely oblivious to that idea. My mindset was different. My mindset was that they were taking from me. They weren't invested into me as a person. I was a commodity. Our coaches wouldn't discipline the star recruits on the team, they would pamper them. They would pacify them. They had to. Their job was on the line. If they don't win, then they get fired and replaced. This wasn't High School sports, this was a business. Parents paid for their kids to make the team by donating money to the school. That tarnished things. Guys who wouldn't make a basketball team otherwise were given spots at the end of the bench. Spots that kids from my neighborhood deserved. That day it was important to show my worth. To show that I'm valuable. When tryouts was over, I left the court, went straight to my locker and began to clear it out. I took my name plate off, packed up everything and left without speaking to anyone. A few days later, the coach sent word through another player that if I wanted to play on the team I still could play, I just had to come and talk to him. Ask me if I went to talk to him. On second thought, don't ask me. It should be clear that I didn't. It bothers me, even to this day, when people try to hold things over your head, give you ultimatums to try and get you to do what they want you to do. My father did that to me for years. I conquered that mountain and was relentless to relinquish that power and give people the impression that they could try to dictate my life.

Now that basketball was no longer my dream, I turned my sights to my new passion, Money, Money, Money, Money, Mon-nay! Mon-nay! My first job was slanging roast beef at Ardy's during my Junior year I still had practice and games to play so I didn't work as much. Now that that was out of the way, I focused on working as much as possible. Working was just like anything else in my life, I put my total effort into it. This time my efforts literally paid off. No longer did I have to take a trip to my Aunt's house to get my cousin's hand me downs or sneak and wear my brothers clothes. I began to accumulate my own. Having money was a way to feed my materialistic dreams. Money doesn't buy certain forms of happiness but it does buy that happiness I experienced when I bought those white on white Jordan 12s I had always wanted since 6th grade when Mike got on the school bus wearing them. I remember just wishing I could afford them. Now I could so I made up for lost time. We would cut school to go to the mall and buy whatever Jordan's came out that day then show up at lunch with them on. It was superficial but I loved getting the attention. Money gave me a new outlet of expression and independence.

With independence, I began to want to understand life and decipher which aspect of life I should adapt to and which part I should shun. Throughout my life, I had heard enough of what others felt I should do. Rarely did I feel like what I was told was factual. The things I was told were never the truth. The truth was always filtered. I began to search for that unfiltered truth.These were the years of my first introduction to freedom. My first introduction into fully thinking from myself instead of doing what people expected or wanted me to do. In my quest for knowledge and truth, my rebellion continued to persist. This led to frequent altercations between me and my father. My resentment for him had accumulated and reached it's tipping point.

My household presented two completely different dynamics. Me and my father didn't get along but I would go to hell and back for my mom and have no problems professing that I'm a mama's boy. It was an odd position for her to be put in. Her husband and her son both resented him. My father is 10 times more stubborn than me and even when he's wrong, he won't admit it so because my mom defended me the majority of the time, it made him resent her and they would argue over me. This only made me resent him more. He knew I didn't need him so there wasn't any consequences to come with me speaking up to him. I considered it making up for lost time. My dad had zero intentions of ever respecting me as a person or even as man. He was devoted to using bible verses to justify why we should listen to what he says. As my hearing diminished, so did our relationship. That crack in our father-son relationship continued to expand. My writing began to expand also.

Before I quit basketball, before I fell in love with money, I fell in love with a girl. We met my Junior year in a class we shared together. There wasn't a fairy tale love at first sight moment but I found her attractive. After a few months of getting to know each other we made it official on April 8th, 2001. We were the Ballard High School version of Jlo and Diddy. We were so cheesy, we would talk on the phone and determine what we were going to wear to school, I would walk her to all her classes and wait for her after class. Typical high school sweetheart stuff. This was nothing like my 12 year old love with Nia. This was more advanced, this was deeper. It was like I had found the one. She was the Love Of My Life.

Unlike when I had to change from one middle school to another middle school changing from Ballard High School to Western Kentucky University was celebrated and welcomed with open arms. That Fall of 2002 was the epitome of freedom. No parents. No supervisions. I took full advantage to this, to my own detriment. I finished that first semester with a 1.6 GPA. Parties took precedence over going to class, especially classes where attendance wasn't a priority and didn't count against you. In college, they give you that freedom to essentially fail on your own. Not going to classes isn't a benefit, but when you're punch drunk with freedom not having to go to class is an awesome thing until it comes time to take test and you lack the knowledge to be successful. I found out the hard way. I found out that long distance relationships don't work either. WKU was only a hour and a half south of Louisville. Having a girlfriend that I loved should have been reason enough to want to go home every weekend but it wasn't. We went from seeing each other almost everyday to seeing each other every few weeks or once a month. That's a drastic change to get used to. In hindsight, I should've went home more. A part of me took her for granted. I knew I loved her and knew I'd marry her, I just negated telling her that or even taking it a step further and showing her that. The fact that I didn't make going home a priority could have been taken as my lack of interest in seeing her but it was moreso about my lack of wanting to be home. It was either go home and have to deal with arguing with your dad and being in a house where the energy was always off or stay in college and hang out with your friends. Roberta got caught in the middle.

For years, my goal was to not only escape that house but to escape Louisville. It was never my intention to go to a College close to home. The University of Miami or USC were my dream schools. I expected to end up at one of those schools, surely never intended to stay in Kentucky. Then I met my Jlo and had to give up my bad boy hopes and dreams. My dream job was to work at ESPN and be just like Stuart Scott. Aside from that I wanted to become a cameraman because I noticed that at all exciting and great events there were cameramen. It'd be a nice way to make it to Super Bowls and NBA games. WKU had a really good Broadcast and Journalism school so while going there was a compromise it wasn't that bad of a compromise. Sometimes compromise is just a quick fix.

Eventually that quick fix ran it's course, we tried hard to make it work but she just came to the conclusion that after 3-ish years we were better off apart. I came to the conclusion that I wanted to kill myself. Heartbreak is the worst possible emotional pain to endure. We went months without even speaking. I never wanted to accept that it was over. I never wanted to accept that everything I expected to happen would never happen. I never wanted to accept the fact that it was all my fault. My pain helped me discover yet another new passion of mine, Poetry. I couldn't talk to her so I wrote to her. I remember we had went months without speaking or seeing each other then one day during winter break when I was back in town. She came over and I showed her the poems I had written about her. The first thing I wrote was a short poem confessing my love for her while we were still together. After we broke up I started with a few poems about the devastation. My life was based around her. Without her what would my life mean? I wasn't ready to figure that out. It wasn't obvious to me at the time but that heartbreak led to immediate depression. I became overcome with guilt and blamed myself for everything that went wrong. That guilt combined with unfulfilled expectations and promises, my pending academic probation became a burden. This was adversity that I had never faced. Adversity that I used my creativity to escape. I used my creativity to heal. I used my creativity to cope. I used creativity to kill myself.

11/29/03

You Tell Me

I'M FLOATING FACE DOWN IN A SEA OF STRESS
GOD BLESS ME
FLOATING DEVICES WOULDN'T DO ME JEST
IT MUST BE
KARMA GETTING BACK AT ME FOR ALL THE WRONG I DID
I PROMISE IF I COULD'VE PREVENTED IT
YOU WOULDN'T HAVE TO GO THROUGH THIS
NOT SINCE THE DEATH OF LOVED ONES HAVE I FELT SUCH PAIN
VISIONS OF BETTER DAYS DANCE AROUND IN MY BRAIN
TRY TO MAINTAIN
IT'S GOING TO GET BETTER
I'M DOWN TO DO WATEVER
TO INSURE YOU JOY
OH BOY
DON'T LET US FALL OFF NOW
WE'VE CAME TOO FAR TO TURN AROUND
I'VE MADE MISTAKES TAKE A BREAK TO HEAR MY HEART
DON'T ACCEPT THE END HOW'S ABOUT A FRESH START
UPS AND DOWNS
HIGHS AND LOWS
IS ALL WE KNOW
WHY NOT HOP IN A CAR HEAD DOWN A STEADY ROAD
IT'S NOT HARD TO KEEP THE GOOD AND FORGET THE BAD
PUT IT ALL IN A BAG
CONSIDER IT TRASH
MY EMOTIONS ARE PURE
YOU BROUGHT HAPPINESS I'VE NEVER FELT BEFORE
AT NIGHT I PRAY TO THE LORD
THAT HE KEEPS OUR LOVE
THAT YOU CONTINUE TO LIKE ME
ON THE DAYS IT DOESN'T SEEM SO LIKELY
BREAK-UPS TO MAKE-UPS
THAT'S THE TALE OF THE TAPE

LET'S DO THINGS DIFFERENTLY STARTING AT TODAY'S PACE
I'M IN IT FOR THE LONG HAUL
I'VE NEVER BEEN ONE TO STALL
I CREATE AND MAKE MOVES
DON'T PLAY GAMES TO LOSE
BUT IN THESE TIMES WHAT'S A YOUNG MAN TO DO??
L.O.V.E. SPELLS BOTH PLEASURE AND PAIN
I MEAN, ONE WORD CAN MEAN TWO DIFFERENT THINGS
I'VE SEEN GOOD TURN TO BAD IN THE BLINK OF AN EYE
MAYBE YOU CAN ANSWER MY HOWS AND WHY
MY BRAINS RATTLED I CAN'T DENY IT
IF YOUR SOULS LOST I CAN HELP YOU FIND IT
MAYBE I'M TOO OPTIMISTIC
MAYBE THERE'S SOMETHING I'M MISSING
IT'S BEEN HOT IN THE KITCHEN
I AIN'T BEEN PAYING ATTENTION
OR AT LEAST NOT LIKE I THOUGHT I WAS
WE SHARED 4 LETTERS WITHOUT KNOWING WHAT IT DOES
TO THE PSYCHE OF A SANE PERSON
ONCE SMALL PROBLEMS TURN INTO BIGGER VERSIONS
AND IT FORCED YOU TO CHANGE
SO I GUESS YOU'RE NOT THE SAME PERSON

YOU TELL ME.

12/12/03

UNFULFILLED PROMISES

MY LIFE'S A POINTLESS MATH PROBLEM
IT AMOUNTS TO NOTHING
I'VE TRIED TO STAND FOR SOMETHING
NO MATTER HOW HARD I TRY
I GET LOST IN THE RUNNING
I'M NOT A CANDIDATE, NOR IS THIS A DEBATE
I FEEL TIME SLIPPING, IT'S GETTING LATE
WHILE I'M NOT SUICIDAL
THERE ARE CATS THAT'S DEALT WITH MORE THAN I'VE BEEN
THROUGH
BUT WHY NOT TAKE THE EASY WAY OUT?
GUIDE MYSELF THROUGH THE BRIGHT LIGHT
MY CONSCIENCE KEEPS ME GROUNDED AND KEEPS ME SANE
SOMETHING'S GOTTA CHANGE
NOT LIKE A NAME
I'VE GOTTA FIND MY WAY OUT OF THIS DARK VORTEX
DEAR GOD, SHINE SOME LIGHT GIVE ME INSIGHT ON WHAT TO
DO NEXT
I'M GRATEFUL FOR THOSE WHO HE'S PLACED AROUND ME
ALIENATION IS A DESTINATION THAT WOULD DROWN ME
NO ONE KNOWS OR UNDERSTANDS WHO I AM
I'VE BEEN SECOND-GUESSED
LABELED SOMETHING OTHER THAN WHAT I AM
WITH NO ONE OR NOWHERE TO RUN TO
OF COURSE I'M LOST MY HEART GROWS COLDER
IF ONLY IT WOULD DEFROST
AN AMOUNT OR BALANCE IS WORTH THE COST
MY AMBITIONS HAVE WRITTEN CHECKS REALITY WON'T CASH
I'VE TRIED TO GET AHEAD
BUT ALWAYS MANAGED TO STUMBLE BACK
MY DRIVE AND DETERMINATION HASN'T SURRENDERED ANY
SLACK
WHAT'S REALLY CONSIDERED BEING A FAILURE

AM I DESTINED?
IF THAT'S THE CASE I'D RATHER SPEND THE REST OF MY LIFE'S
CYCLE RESTING.

12/13/03

INSOMNIA

I FINALLY CONFRONTED MY UNDERLYING EMOTION
MY PAIN RUNS DEEPER THAN THE DEEPEST OCEAN
WITH MY EYES CLOSED
I PRAY AND BEGIN HOPING
THAT GOD CLOSE CLOSE DOWN WHAT WAS ONCE OPEN
I NEED THE STRENGTH OF TEN MEN
TO HANDLE THE WEIGHT I FEEL ON MY SHOULDERS
YESTERDAY IS A FAVORABLE OUTCOME
INSTEAD OF WAITING TIL I'M OLDER
IF I'M GONE, I'M ASSURED I'D BE MISSED
BEING WITHOUT HOPE IS A DISEASE I WISH DIDN'T EXIST
WHAT'S WRITTEN ON THIS SLAB OF OAK WOOD IS EASILY
MISUNDERSTOOD
NOT EVEN I CAN DECIPHER WHAT'S WRITTEN IN THESE LINES
EVEN THOUGH THEY COME FROM THESE
EYES
EARS
HANDS
MOUTH
HEART OF MINES
IS WHAT TOMORROW HOLDS EVEN WORTH THE QUESTIONS?
THE ANSWER HASN'T AMASSED AND I'M TIRED OF GUESSING
THEY SAY LIFE'S A TEST, WELL I WISH I HAD A CHEAT SHEET
A FALSE HOPE ISN'T ENOUGH TO GET ME WHERE I WANT TO BE
I'M TRAPPED IN A MAZE
I'VE BEEN SHIELDED FROM THE LIGHT FOR DAYS
WHEN'S MY DAY GONNA COME?
WILL MY LIFE BE CONSIDERED A WASTE?
DREAMS NEVER DIE
THINK OF ME WHEN YOU CRY
REMEMBER THE GOOD ABOUT ME BEFORE I TOOK THAT RIDE
NEVER LOOK DOWN, KEEP YOUR HEAD HELD UP HIGH
I'VE BEEN APPOINTED TO RESIDE IN THE SKY.

In Loving Memory of

Emmanuel Daniel Clack
1984-2003

EPILOGUE

Location: Los Angeles, CA
Date: May 1, 2016
Time: 12:28pm PST

6 years ago I encountered so many skeptics
6 years later who would of guessed it
6 years from now what's to be expected?
6 years ago I took a leap
6 years later I landed here
friends from 6 years ago are the voices I never hear
the faces I never see
6 years later new sounds and sights surround me
6 years ago they judged me
6 years later, strangers are the ones who love me.
Infatuated, intrigued and interested into the life I lead
not never knowing 6 years ago I wasn't this person.
6 years ago I created this version
6 years ago I wasn't impressed, wasn't motivated enough
so I altered my lifestyle so that 6 years later I'd be where I'm at now
Constantly moving rarely taking time to sit down
Long nights and early morning, the sacrifice of stability doesn't seem
    worth it
6 years ago I was far from perfect
6 years later I'm perfected
The man God had expected
heavy belief, strong with my faith like a rosary necklace
6 years ago I ceased to exist in the spiritual sense
gave my physical being in exchange for a new spirit
might sound awkward to hear it

The person from 6 years ago is no longer present
6 years later, it's something greater that I represent
Think the movie Ghost
When another being enters another being
able to guide that person in a different context
on the interior and exterior is opposite
6 years ago I bowed to my transgressions
my fears and doubts in exchange for a new beginning
6 years later, I've mastered living
never forgetting my purpose
so to answer your question
it's well worth it
6 years ago I didn't sleep out of uncertainty
6 years later I find rest in places most wouldn't certainly be.
6 years ago my load was heavy
metaphorically speaking of the cross I was bearing
6 years later, I learned how to bear it
Now it weighs on me less
6 years ago I prayed that 6 years later I'd be where I'm at
without a destination in mind
just constantly in search of the best ways to lend my time
6 years ago, suicide always on the back burner
served as my default
6 years later, I stand in the face of my fault
all my battles been fought
hearing lessons of the things I've been taught
6 years ago, you could of moved me
6 years later, nothing moves me
my life is a movie
this role fits me best
this scene is the best picture
they act as if I can't see it
like I'm not cut from a different cloth
willing to stick to the script at all cost
no rewards from awards you don't need to win
6 years ago, I completed the first phase
6 years later, I've expanded the stage

switched levels, gears and increased the gage
this is the man I raised
no quarrels of dying at an early age
the good die young
how old do I have to be to fit that notion?
6 years ago you didn't know me
6 years later, you've stumbled onto a book I left open
hoping that 6 years from now it affects you
that it helps you, grateful for those who
6 years ago offered advice support encouragement and help too
6 years later doing my part to continue the cycle
living scriptures from my bible
I say mine because it's as I interpreted it
reading these lines there might be more than my intent that you get
    from it
let's live in abundance
no worries of fear
it's expected to be the first who did it
never let apprehension cloud your vision
6 years ago I did
6 years later, I'm glad I did it
it's not what you're going through
more about how you got through it
how you never gave up
how you stuck to your guns
6 years from now, I'll speak of times from 12 years ago lord willin
took 26 years for me to challenge myself in order to figure out who I am
32 years ago my parents gave birth to a life I now lead
6 years later, thanks to the 26 days that changed my life 6 years ago
6 years ago I took a trip
6 years later, I'm noticing it was a journey
not an experiment
life experience
not a choice
but by chance, nothing you plan
ever goes as planned
learned to adjust

to adapt
to find my way
learned to not give up
challenged myself to grow
challenged myself to evolve
not to stay stagnant but to rapidly progress
it wasn't a few days but an entire process
looking back astonished and proud that I made it
amazed at the distance I've came since
finding things common in the things that don't make sense
what makes us different is what makes us all alike
enabled with the ability to fight
just have to choose wisely, I let my faith guide me
to sights unseen
walls of trust built on notions of the visions made without my eyes
    open
A celebration for my culmination, these are the days I stayed up nights
    for
the times I lost track of times
fixated with the task of reaching my purpose
it doesn't take things breaking to realize things aren't working
strived to fix my broken path
life is temporary
so I studied how to leave an impact that'll last
appreciation to those when in times we shared a smile, hug or laugh
never forgetting the strife
continued apologies for those I've angered
my promise is that my heart is never missing
it's forever in the right position
I'm humbled to have the opportunity to share and elaborate upon my
    fate
Looking back I was always looking forward in anticipation of these
    encounters
tipping the scale in the search of balance
accepting the challenge, accumulating mileage
6 years in the making
look how far I made it

memories made as the old ones fade
new version of my once self
fell in love with me
couldn't wait on someone else.

Made in the USA
Columbia, SC
13 October 2018